EVERYTHING WE NEED

HIS STRENGTH FOR OUR JOURNEY

Ginger Millermon

ANOTHEN MUSIC™

TABLE OF CONTENTS

"We are afflicted in every way, but not crushed; perplexed, but not driven to despair;
Persecuted, but not forsaken; struck down, but not destroyed."
2 Corinthians 4:8-9

"If we cannot believe God when circumstances
seem to be against us, we do not
believe Him at all."
Charles Spurgeon

The shrill ringing of the phone jarred me from sleep. As I rolled over pain, shot through my abdomen from my recent cesarean section. I had only been released from the hospital the night before. We had reluctantly left our premature twins in the Neonatal Intensive Care Unit (NICU) for a few hours so I could get some rest. I heard Joel quietly answer the phone. His tone quickly turned to one of alarm and I knew the news was not good.

"What? How soon?" His eyes met mine and we both began to tear up. "Ok," he replied into the phone. "We are on our way."

He took me into his arms and broke the news. "Jarrott's getting worse. They have to transfer him to Denver this morning. The plane is on its way from Children's Hospital"— he paused—"and only one of us can go with him."

I sobbed in complete exhaustion. I wasn't anywhere close to recovered from my surgery and knew there was no way I could travel the 250 miles to Denver. Besides that obstacle, Jarrott's twin, our other preemie son, Brennan, would still be in the hospital closer to our home. I needed to be with him.

We quickly dressed and raced the seventy-miles to the hospital. The doctor had emphasized on the phone that Jarrott was deathly ill. I knew there was a very good possibility that he would not survive and I would not see him again. We barely made it to the NICU in time as the flight crew prepared Jarrott's incubator and stabilized him for the flight. He was so fragile I wasn't even allowed to touch him. I had never held him in my arms. Any touch or contact overstimulated his tiny body and sent his heart racing out of control. Tears streaming down my face, I leaned as close as I could and told him goodbye, whispering my love for him. I shook in fear and grief as I watched them roll his incubator away.

Life is hard. And it never turns out the way we think it will. We stubbornly try to do it all on our own, and we fail. We often refuse to acknowledge our weaknesses and determine to pull ourselves up by our bootstraps and independently forge ahead. But we weren't made to do it on our own; we were made to depend on a Creator Who loves us. We need the power of Jesus working in our lives to have strength for the long journey ahead.

There is a reason you have picked up this book. Maybe you are going through a life-changing trial. Maybe you are simply struggling to breathe and get through the day. Perhaps you are seeking help for a loved one who is suffering. Whatever the reason, this is true: we all need God's strength more than ever. In an increasingly ungodly culture and with economic and political crises seeming to loom around every corner, we must come to a place of realizing that we can't victoriously walk through this life on our own. We need help far beyond our limited abilities.

I have survived trials I couldn't have imagined. But God's grace has been sufficient, and He has taught me things I never would have learned otherwise. On this side of very deep valleys, I am immensely grateful for the things our family endured because walking through the fire has allowed us to experience God's unfailing faithfulness. Enduring tragedies and hardship has brought me to the end of myself so many times, and that's when God's best work has been done in my heart.

Recently a woman came to me after a women's conference and wept as she told me about her son, a boy in his early teens, who had walked away from God and their family. The last she had heard he was living on the streets, and she hadn't seen him in months. Her eyes welling with tears, she asked, "Why? Why is God allowing this to happen? I tried to do everything right. I've tried to be a good parent." My heart broke for her as we cried together.

I'm not going to pretend to have all the answers. In fact, outside of the wisdom of God's Word, I have nothing to offer you at all. I can simply present biblical truths, examples and promises from God's Word, and tell you what He's done in my life and in the lives of others through trials. I'm sure there are hundreds more reasons we suffer than I can list, but here are a few things I've come to realize.

> There are times when He will use seasons of intense suffering to bring us back to our senses.

These times may come after we have walked away and decided we could do this life on our own. I have discovered that when my life is clicking along and things are running smoothly, it is easy to get lazy, shorten my time of prayer, or skip it altogether. God's Word can quickly become less precious and after a short Psalm or Proverb of the day, off I go to conquer my world. Many times I have felt the gentle, loving reminder that I'm trying to do things *for* Him...*without* Him! I have been humbled enough times to know I can't walk out my front door without messing something up. D.L. Moody said it beautifully when he stated,

> "In the divine partnership, we contribute weakness."

Basically, we've got nothing. We need Him.

In addition to my own struggles, there have been people I loved dearly at various times throughout my life who have needed that wake-up call from God. Maybe you have prayed this for a loved one. It is a bold prayer. "God, would You do *whatever it takes* to get their attention? Would You open their eyes and bring them back?"

You had better be ready when you pray that! It's a little scary, isn't it? Especially if you realize that perhaps someone is praying that prayer over you! I have prayed that specific prayer with fear and trembling over several loved ones in my life. And I have seen God do amazing things. He uses trials to make us wholly and utterly rely on Him, to remind us of His love, and bring us back to His feet. I have learned the very most and experienced the sweetest care by my Savior in my times of deepest suffering.

Sometimes we suffer because of our own sin and poor choices.

Now, I know this is stating the obvious, but honestly, a lot of the things we gripe about we bring on ourselves. We suffer the pain of our sin, and even when we have sought restitution and forgiveness, there are natural consequences for our actions. Whether it's gossip that breaks down a friendship, lust, infidelity, or selfishness that destroys a marriage, or unwise spending and debt creating stress, there are endless times when our sin results in hardship. God will use even those times in our lives to teach us, mature us, and change us. But not all hardship is due to sin of my own.

Sometimes we suffer simply because we live in a fallen, sinful world.

Ever since the Garden of Eden and the Fall of Man, there has been sin in this world and we all suffer from it. I remember as small child, first learning about Creation and the whole fiasco with Adam and Eve and the serpent in the Garden. I recall in my very immature mind being really put out with them. I mean, really...just say no. Tell the snake to get lost. That's all they had to do. But no, they ate the fruit and blew it for the rest of us! It seemed wrong to me. And as a kid, I was *sure* if it had been me, I would have responded so differently and the world would still be paradise. What unbelievable pride on my part! As I grew in knowledge of God's Word and recognized my own wicked, sinful heart, I knew I wouldn't have done anything differently than Adam and Eve. In fact, I probably would have had two pieces of fruit.

There is no way around the consequences of the Fall of Man. It's not going to be solved until Jesus takes us home. But until then, we will suffer illness, weariness, hard work, broken relationships, and death.

Several years ago when we were on tour with our kids, we stopped at the Creation Museum in Petersburg, Kentucky. What an amazing experience! As we walked through the museum with videos portraying the days of Creation, displays of dinosaurs and other exotic, fantastic creatures, we reached a point in the tour that featured a diorama of the Garden of Eden. We saw Adam and Eve in paradise with animals, beautiful trees, and flowers surrounding them. As we continued to walk, we saw Eve engaged in conversation with the slimy serpent who was hanging down from a tree. Next, we saw the results of the Fall as, clothed in animal skins, they toiled in the dirt. But what made the greatest impression on us was rounding a corner and seeing a wooden door covered in graffiti. We walked through a narrow room plastered with images of the Holocaust, war, drugs, and death. The visual was clear. As soon as the Fall occurred, the beautiful, perfect world that God created was no more. Instead, with each generation, things grew more corrupt, more evil, and more godless. We can't escape it. So we must look to our great source of hope...God's Word.

"His divine power has granted to us all things that pertain to life and godliness, through the knowledge of him who called us to his own glory and excellence, by which he has granted to us his precious and very great promises, so that through them you may become partakers of the divine nature, having escaped from the corruption that is in the world because of sinful desire." 2 Peter 1:3-4

We have all the resources, all the power we need! It's right at our fingertips in God's Word. We don't need talk shows, advice columns, Oprah, or the New York Times bestseller list to figure things out and survive our circumstances. You don't need this book you're holding right now. You only need *the* Book. Through His divine, unfathomable power, He will give you everything you need. He knows all about you. He should...He created you. He loves you, He treasures you, and He can rescue you.

In the second chapter of his second book, Peter reminds his readers about Lot's circumstances in Sodom. Lot had made poor choices about where he was living, and with whom he was keeping company. Even so, God, in His great mercy, rescued Lot at the last minute before Sodom and Gomorrah were judged and incinerated with fire from heaven. As Peter finishes telling Lot's story he says,

"...then the Lord knows how to rescue the godly from trials." 2 Peter 2:9

And Peter should know! He was writing 1 and 2 Peter at a time of extreme persecution against the church. Nero was marking the beginning of his reign with a relentless, bloody crusade against Christians, hunting them down and torturing them in unspeakable ways. In fact, there is historical documentation that Nero was having fires set in Rome and blaming the Christians so that he could incense and motivate the public to expose and turn in the followers of Christ. Men, women, and children were being thrown to the lions, butchered, and torn apart for entertainment in the coliseums. Nero was even using the Christians as human torches to illuminate his garden paths.

In light of all this, listen to Peter's words.

"Beloved, do not be surprised at the fiery trial when it comes upon you to test you, as though something strange were happening to you. But rejoice insofar that you share Christ's sufferings, that you may also rejoice and be glad when his glory is revealed."
1 Peter 4:12-13

When Peter talked about persecution and trials, he was drawing directly from his own experiences. He had been beaten, jailed, and threatened. In this passage, he was challenging the Jewish Christians, who were being driven out of Jerusalem and spread across Asia Minor, to not be shocked that they were going through trials, as though something totally unexpected were happening. I love that part of the verse. I need to be reminded that painful trials aren't really anything unusual. They are a part of this life that God uses to refine us and lead us to holiness and sanctification—to be set apart for Him and to be more Christlike. Hardship and trials are used by God to mold us ever more into the image of His Son. Peter is encouraging the early church to be prepared. Trials will come.

If I really stop and think about it, I get pretty dismayed thinking about my responses when things don't go my way. How many times have I exclaimed, "Can't anything go right? Could this day get any worse?" Well, yes, as a matter of fact, it could. If I would check the news online for ten seconds, it would become pretty clear that many people are having a much worse day than I am! Not coincidentally, as I started writing this book, our ladies Bible study in my church was reading through *Foxe's Book of Martyrs*. It was a sobering time for me to assess my own life and commitment, a time to weep for those who have gone before us in willing suffering and martyrdom to further the cause of Christ and the gospel. It challenges me greatly in the way I view the difficult moments and seasons of my own life. Over and over I read accounts of men who humbly, even cheerfully, went to the stake to be burned. Men who happily pulled the burning sticks closer, crying out, "More fire!" They truly felt honored and privileged to give their lives for the truth of the gospel.

I am ashamed to admit how easily I find myself getting discouraged and derailed in my day-to-day circumstances. I get caught up in trying to figure out why something is happening, wallowing in a pity party. I don't have to know why. I don't have to figure it all out. All I really have to know is that God is good, He is in control, and He has a reason for all things (Rom. 8:28).

Peter was encouraging these courageous believers to not focus on the trial, but to focus on rejoicing that they were able to participate in Christ's suffering. They were actually being persecuted solely for their faith in Jesus. They were getting a tiny taste, a glimpse of all He had suffered for them when He was scorned, beaten, and crucified. Again, it shames me. My trials are *nothing* compared to what my Savior endured for me. They are nothing compared to what these precious people were facing. They were running for their lives, watching their children be murdered, hiding for years in underground tunnels. And I think I'm having a "trial" when my car breaks down or my computer crashes or my coffeemaker dies? Indeed, there are many inconveniences in life to be sure, but sometimes I need a reality check. Reading through 1 and 2 Peter will do it! I realize that many who are reading this are going through real, deep, and devastating trials. What hope the writings of Peter bring us! As he was addressing the trials his readers were experiencing, he gave this positive aspect of suffering:

"In this you rejoice, though now for a little while, if necessary, you have been grieved by various trials, so that the tested genuineness of your faith—more precious than gold that perishes though it is tested by fire—may be found to result in praise and glory and honor at the revelation of Jesus Christ." 1 Peter 1:6-7

Peter declared our faith of greater beauty and value than

gold. However, in order to be beautiful and valuable, gold has to be refined. This is a complex process of heating up, melting down, and purifying the precious metal. As gold is heated, impurities surface and become removable, resulting in a purer product. When gold goes through the fire, the junk floats to the top. The same is true in our lives. Many times when things start to heat up, God will use that fire to expose sin and attitudes that have been tucked away in a secret place, sin that needs to be dealt with and purged.

This refining process happened in a big way for me. Joel and I had been married for several years before our daughter McKenzie arrived. Joel was a youth pastor in the beautiful little coal-mining town in Colorado where he had grown up. We loved the ministry God had allowed us to be a part of, and we absolutely loved being new parents. Life was good. On McKenzie's first birthday, we were thrilled to find out we were expecting again. We had no idea what was in store for us. Twenty-nine weeks into our pregnancy, we were shocked to learn we were expecting twin boys! Only a few days later they arrived, ten weeks early and fighting for their lives. Brennan and Jarrott were tiny, two pounds, fourteen ounces, apiece and barely over a foot long. Brennan was what the doctors called a "grower." He simply needed to keep his body temperature up, learn to eat and breathe at the same time, and he could come home. He was healthy enough by two months old to be released from the NICU on oxygen and monitors. It was a fairly typical preemie course for him.

Jarrott was an entirely different story. Although the boys looked identical, Jarrott was born with severe chronic lung and airway disease. That's why, four days after birth, Jarrott was airlifted over the mountains to Denver. This was only the beginning of a long, painful journey for our family. When I said goodbye to him at four days old, I truly thought I would not see him alive again. When he reached Children's Hospital, they put him on a different life support system and managed to stabilize him temporarily. It was three weeks before my doctor released me to travel to him. Three weeks with Joel and Jarrott suffering on the other side of the Continental Divide, hundreds of miles away. Even when I was finally allowed to travel, my heart was torn because I had to leave Brennan in the hospital on the other side of the mountains. It was a no-win situation. In the middle of all that chaos, we had McKenzie, only eighteen months old, being shuffled between grandparents.

By the time Jarrott was four months old, he had undergone major stomach reconstruction, had a feeding tube inserted into his stomach, and had a tracheotomy so he could continue on life-support. He couldn't eat anything by mouth or breathe without the ventilator. Either Joel or I were almost always at his side, watching over him, praying over him, hoping for him. But he continued to decline, and our doctors were giving up on him. Our boys were born in August and by Christmas that year, it became obvious that Jarrott was probably not going to survive. Right after the holidays, our specialists sat us down and told us that Jarrott had contracted a virus that would most likely be fatal for him. His organs were shutting down, becoming permanently damaged, and he was slipping into a coma.

Then they asked us the unthinkable. They asked us to take him off of life-support, and let him die. It was a nightmare decision no parent should ever have to face. They stated that if, by some miracle, Jarrott survived, he would never walk or talk. He would be on a ventilator and in a wheelchair his whole life. Doctors said he would have severe cerebral palsy and would have no quality of life. Those were their exact words. I will never forget that moment as long as I live. Faced with all of these horrific predictions on Jarrott's life and significant pressure from our doctors, Joel and I still knew we needed to leave him on life support and give him every chance to live. We were left to wait and see if our son would survive. Family was called, and doctors put us into a private room to grieve. Even remaining on life support, his specialists expected that Jarrott would live only a few hours or days at the most. He was dying.

God showed tremendous mercy on our family over the next hours. After the funeral was planned and our good-byes were said, God amazed everyone! At literally the last moment, God miraculously intervened and spared Jarrott's life, beginning the slow process of healing his diseased lungs. Our doctors shook their heads in disbelief more than once as Jarrott defied all the odds. It was a long, hard road for our family. Jarrott was in the NICU for over a year, many of those months spent hundreds of miles from home. When he finally did come home, he was in a wheelchair, on a ventilator with a tracheotomy, and still had a feeding tube. We had twenty-four hour nursing care in our home for years, and that in itself was extremely stressful. It was a painful, hot, refining process for our family.

Shortly after Jarrott came home from the hospital, it became evident to both Joel and me that there were problems and issues in our marriage that needed to be addressed. As Jarrott's health needs lingered on, the stress in our lives continued to grow, and God started to bring those impurities in our family to the surface, much like the heating up of gold in the refinement process. We both agreed that a biblical counselor was needed, and we started regular sessions. I'll never forget one afternoon session in particular as I watched our counselor put up a white board and then draw a huge volcano with smoke and flames spewing out of the top. He turned and looked right at me, pointing to the volcano.

He said, "This is you, and you're going to blow."

Well, that wasn't exactly what I had in mind to hear that day. But he was right. I had major anger and pride issues that had to be resolved. And God used the fire of a long-term illness with our son to heat my life up and force the junk to the surface. Over those months, God opened my eyes to pride, self-righteousness, stubbornness, and a host of other sins. And He started to refine me. Trials are often used by God to refine us, to make us more holy. Purification can be intense and long. Our tendency is to give up and get out of the heat. But there is beauty, sanctification, and transparency on the other side of refining if we will let God do His work. And the best part is when we come through the fire, our faith can be more genuine, more real, and deeper than it's ever been.

What about you? Are you walking through the fire? Are you going to blow? Are you willing to be refined, or are you still scrambling to get out of the heat? I really don't have all the answers to the "why" questions, and I don't understand all the reasons why we suffer. I don't believe we will know all of the reasons until we reach eternity. But God's Word contains tremendous hope. Even though the journey is often painful, it is not fruitless. God has good plans in mind for our lives. He can and will use the circumstances that we go through to produce character, bring about needed change, and increase our sanctification. Whether our trials are a consequence of sin, due to circumstances outside our control, or a result of God refining us, we can rest assured knowing that all are under the sovereignty and control of God. Our suffering will serve a purpose.

So, how are you going to deal with the reality of the trials you will face? You have a choice. You can simply survive—fainthearted, tired, whining, praying every day for the rapture. Or you can grow—facing the heat, embracing the refining, determined for purification, all for the end purpose of bringing glory to God. We will take the rest of the chapters in this book to study and think on what it looks like to have a heart willing to suffer and grow through trials. God has given us so many incredible examples of suffering in His Word where we can glean truths for our personal growth and maturity. I pray that the following pages will be a great comfort and challenge to you as we study biblical examples, and the ultimate and perfect example of suffering that we see in our Savior Jesus Christ.

CHAPTER TWO

A Surrendered Heart

"...for he has said,
'I will never leave you nor forsake you.'
So we can confidently say,
"The Lord is my helper; I will not fear;
what can man do to me?" Heb: 13:5a-6

"No matter what you are facing today you are not alone. The One who still wears your flesh is interceding for you. He knows exactly what it is to suffer as you are and he has promised he will never leave you." Elyse Fitzpatrick

Trials always change us. They alter our perspective and make the little things seem insignificant, at least for a while. Many of us can look back without hesitation to a time in our lives when the big one hit—the fiery trial that made everything else fade into the background. That instant when time shifted into slow motion, life became very focused, and we feared things would never be the same. A middle-of-the-night phone call bringing news of tragedy, a terrifying diagnosis, a spouse declaring they love someone else, or an open window through which your beloved teenager has slipped away. Trials will come, they always do. From the beginning of time and the curse of man in the garden, trials are par for the course, the ebb and flow of this life on earth. We can't escape trials, so how do we deal with them? How we respond matters. What we do with the difficulties and anguish we face in our short time here matters. We don't have to be a slave to our circumstances. Bad things, hard things, happen every day, and we get to choose how we are going to respond. We get to choose our perspective.

I'm always interested in hearing other people's stories. It fascinates me how someone can go through something that, humanly speaking, should have completely devastated them, should have left them in the fetal position permanently, and yet they forge on. I admire their strength and perseverance. Then I hear another story from someone else, whose trial in comparison seems like a broken toe, and yet they are side-lined for years.

I recently saw a heartbreaking news story about a little girl and her family from the Texas Panhandle. It was a re-al-life mystery/crime report about a family who had their home broken into, and all of the family members were killed in the middle of the night except the ten-year-old little girl. She was shot and left for dead along with her family. The sto-ry especially caught my attention because we have an eleven-year-old daughter. I honestly could not imagine something so horrific happening to her. As the tragic story unfolded, I was astounded at the strength of that little girl. There was even original footage of her brave 911 call from outside the house, while she waited for police, and video of her answer-ing questions with a counselor. Her courageous spirit shone through even in those first hours after the gruesome event. She was then featured on the show as a young woman, ten years later. I was astounded by her determination to not let that time in her life define her forever.

Of course, it changed her, devastated her, and robbed her of her precious family and childhood. But she chose to not be a victim forever. She chose to live her life fully in memory and honor of her family. I don't know for certain where she got her strength and courage. The report didn't say whether or not she had a relationship with God; although when inter-viewed, her childhood pastor spoke of her family's devotion and commitment to their church. I *do* know, however, where I get my strength and courage when trials hit, and where we each have promised strength and grace for every need. It's not by pulling ourselves up and determining to do better, cry less, be braver. I've tried all of that at one time or another in my life. No, the strength we find to persevere when the impossible happens, is in God's Word and in our relationship with Him. It's in His promises, His truths, and His precious love letter to us.

> The good news about those fiery trials is that we don't face them alone.
> The best news about trials is that God will use them for our good and His glory.

I mentioned that I love stories. I love stories from history, from current events, and especially from the Bible. I am encouraged to hear accounts of others who have suffered and have done more than simply survived; they have thrived. I am also challenged by stories of those who have suffered and have *not* thrived, responded well, or matured in the refining process. It is good to see both sides of that scenario. It is good to remember that we get to choose our outlook and attitude.

Genesis chapter four contains one of those biblical stories for us to consider. Truly it is the perfect example of a person facing a trial brought on solely by his own doing. It's a familiar story that takes place at the very beginning of time, long before any excuses such as peer pressure, TV, or culture could be employed. Adam and Eve were the first parents and had been kicked out of paradise because of their sin. They had gone from a perfect life and intimate fellowship with God, to living outside the Garden of Eden and facing hardship at every turn. Nothing was easy anymore.

Cain and Able were the first children born under the curse. They knew where their parents' sin had taken them, and what their life was like before. In spite of this foreknowledge, Cain plowed ahead with the family legacy of foolishness, and rejected God's plan. Immediately after the devastating account of the Fall of man, we read the tragic story of Cain and Abel. It is astounding how quickly sin escalated once it entered the world!

God required a sacrifice of Cain and Able. Cain was a farmer and brought portions from his crops. Abel was a shepherd and brought the firstborn of his flock for an offering. The Bible says that God looked with favor and acceptance on Abel's offering, but He did not look with favor on Cain's offering. Now, it doesn't say in Genesis exactly why God did not approve of Cain's offering, but God must have certainly informed Adam and his family how to approach Him and what was required for a sacrifice. Hebrews 9:22 says that without blood being shed, there is no remission of sin. But Cain brought a bloodless offering from the fruit of his farming. His offering was not accepted, perhaps because it was not a blood offering or because of a lack of faith or a wrong motive.[1]

Hebrews 11:4 offers some insight:

"By faith Abel offered to God a more acceptable sacrifice than Cain, through which he was commended as righteous, God commending him by accepting his gifts. And through his faith, though he died, he still speaks." Heb. 11:4

The bottom line is this, Abel's offering was acceptable, and Cain's was not. Abel offered his gift in faith, was a righteous man, God was pleased, and accepted his sacrifice. Cain's sacrifice did not meet God's approval, and Cain was mad. That's when things really went downhill for Cain. The amazing thing to me about this story is that God offered Cain an opportunity to change. As I've mentioned, we get to choose our perspective, our attitude, when situations in life don't go the way we expect. Cain had that same opportunity. God even reminded Cain of that choice.

God asked Cain, "Why are you angry, and why has your face fallen?" The Revised English Bible reads, "Why are you scowling?" God went on to remind Cain that if he would do the right thing he would be accepted.

The Lord said to Cain, "Why are you angry, and why has your face fallen? If you do well, will
you not be accepted? And if you do not do well, sin is crouching at the door.
Its desire is for you, but you must rule over it." Gen. 4:6-7

God clearly offered Cain the opportunity to receive His approval, to make a change. Cain could have turned things around, recovered from this sin, this trial he had created for himself, if he had chosen to do the right thing. I love the wording in those verses, that sin is "crouching at the door." That word picture is so vivid and so true! Sin is always right around the corner, and we are faced with a choice of how we will respond. We have the option, much like Cain, to choose to submit and surrender to God's plan for us, or to continue to try to do things our own way.

God so beautifully demonstrated His merciful patience with sinful man in this dramatic biblical exchange. God took note of Cain's anger and scowling countenance. Before Cain said a word, God knew his heart. Our sinful attitudes and inward motives don't escape God's notice either. Those things we secretly harbor in our hearts are open to God's inspection. Unlike limited man, God sees the full condition of our hearts and completely understands our actions and attitudes (Prov. 16:2). In fact, He knows our hearts better than we know ourselves. God saw Cain's deep-seated rebellion. Even if Cain had given the "right" offering, God knew his motives were impure. Even so, He gave Cain the chance to repent. Cain rejected God's word, God's advice to him, and he walked away from the presence of the Lord.

Well, you know the story. Instead of owning up to his sin and changing his attitude, Cain refused to submit his will to God. He was intent on doing things his own way. Unchecked, the only way sin was naturally going to go was downhill! It will always go from bad to worse.

Cain spoke to Abel his brother. And when they were in the field,
Cain rose up against his brother Abel and killed him. Gen. 4:8

Now that was some serious bad attitude! Cain's disappointment in God's disfavor snowballed quickly into anger, jealousy, and murder. Cain had absolutely no reason to be angry with Abel. Pure jealousy fueled his anger. 1 John 3:12 tells us Cain killed Abel simply because he was evil, and Abel was righteous. I am reminded when I read Cain's story that those "little" sins of anger, jealousy, and discontentment will always keep growing if they aren't put to death. One of my favorite passages about Christian living is found in Colossians 3 where we are told to "put to death" or to kill sin in our lives. One of the sins listed is anger. We can't ignore the seriousness and consequences of allowing anger to take root and grow in our hearts. Cain paid a high price for giving place to his anger!

> Then the Lord said to Cain, "Where is Abel your brother?" He said, "I do not know; am I my brother's keeper?" And the Lord said, "What have you done? The voice of your brother's blood is crying to me from the ground. And now you are cursed from the ground, which has opened its mouth to receive your brother's blood from your hand. When you work the ground, it shall no longer yield to you its strength. You shall be a fugitive and a wanderer on the earth." Cain said to the Lord, "My punishment is greater than I can bear. Gen. 4:9-13

For the rest of his life Cain wandered the earth, a farmer who could never get a crop to grow again. We would do well to learn from his experience! Often we are so stubborn that when we make mistakes, instead of owning up to them, we deny and hide them, letting our sin fester and grow. Will we see our sin and repent, surrendering our will to God's will? Cain walked away, ignoring God's words to him and shunning the opportunity to have God's favor. What a horrible way to spend his life. Oh, that we would learn from Cain's mistakes!

While we can learn how *not* to respond from Cain, I am so encouraged to find, in the same book of Genesis, a beautiful story of a surrendered, obedient heart that God greatly used. Let's consider the amazing life of Joseph.

Genesis chapters 37-50 chronicle the tale of Joseph, the great-grandson of Abraham, one of Jacob's twelve sons, and his father's obvious favorite child. Joseph's father gave him a coat of many colors fit for a king. Some commentators even say Joseph's elaborate coat signified that he was chosen as the firstborn heir over all of his older brothers.[2] His brothers harbored deep jealousy and hatred toward Joseph because of that favoritism. Furthermore, if he was being chosen heir over legitimate firstborn Rueben, the tensions must have been high in Jacob's household! While we admire and learn from Joseph's life, he was by no means perfect or sinless. It didn't help the already tense, dysfunctional family when he told them that he had dreams where they all bowed down to him and he ruled over them. Those dreams were going to be fulfilled very literally at a later time, but they were not taken well by the band of brothers!

> **Note to self:** if someone already hates you, use extreme caution when sharing the "someday you are going to bow down to me" dreams!

> **Note to parents:** Don't have a favorite child! If you just can't help it, keep it to yourself!

You can read the details of this incredible story for yourself in Genesis, but here's the setting for the long, unthinkable trial Joseph was to endure. Joseph's brothers hated him so much that the instant they had the opportunity, they got rid of him. At first planning to simply kill him, they changed their minds when they saw a way to not only get rid of their dreamer brother, but to make some quick cash as well. They seemed to feel no remorse as they sold him to slave traders traveling to Egypt, knowing most likely he would not even survive the weeks-long journey through the desert. They knew he would probably be chained and forced to walk those agonizing miles. Later in Genesis, these men talked amongst themselves, and remembered how Joseph had pleaded and begged for his life. Amazing, isn't it, how "innocent" jealousy, anger, and hatred escalated again, as it had with Cain, to a willingness to take a life without hesitation? And not only were they perfectly fine disposing of their younger brother, there was no compassion for the grief they would inflict upon their father! They soaked Joseph's clothes in goat's blood and took it to their father with the callous statement: "This we have found; please identify whether it is your son's robe or not." (Gen. 37:32). Unbelievable!

What hateful, hard hearts! What a painful reminder that our sin will lead us to depths we never imagined we would go. Those wicked, ten sons watched as their father tore his robes, wept bitterly, clothed himself in sackcloth and ashes, and grieved for his beloved son. They never caved, never softened, and never spilled the truth. They simply moved on with their selfish lives while their father mourned, and Joseph suffered, betrayed by his own family, his own flesh and blood.

In the meantime Joseph *did* survive, walking hundreds of miles through the desert as a shackled slave. I was fascinated to read, as I studied commentaries and maps, that the route Joseph must have taken to Egypt as a slave, passed not so far from his home in Hebron.[3] He probably could see the hill country of his homeland less than one hundred miles to the east of the caravan of traders. How unbelievably sad and heartbreaking for this young man! What sinking dread he assuredly felt as he was carried off, farther and farther from his beloved father!

When the caravan reached Egypt, Joseph was likely taken to the slave market. He was sold into the wealthy, opulent household of Potiphar, the captain of Pharaoh's guard. I think if a person *had* to be sold as a slave into a home in ancient Egypt, probably Potiphar's luxurious estate would be a decent place to land. God was putting a perfect plan into motion. It is a beautiful thing to read Genesis, and see God's deliberate care for Joseph when surely all must have seemed lost to him. At only seventeen years old, Joseph found himself isolated and all alone in the world. Snatched away from everyone and everything familiar. Raised as a shepherd in a nomadic existence, Joseph was suddenly thrust into the most sophisticated culture in the world. Can you even imagine what went through his mind as they pulled into busy Egypt, teeming with people and amazing architecture? His situation as a slave in an unfamiliar culture probably felt overwhelming and hopeless.

But look at the first line of Genesis 39:2.

"The Lord was with Joseph…" Gen. 39:2a

What a beautiful reminder that no matter where we go, how far we are from what is familiar, or the people in our lives that keep us accountable and love us, God is ever near. Truly, He will "never leave you nor forsake you" (Heb. 13:5). When everything looks impossible for Joseph in this story, we are reminded of God's presence.

It didn't take Joseph's master long to realize there was something very different about Joseph. Everything Joseph did, everything he touched prospered. He was diligent, hardworking, and conscientious, even as a slave trapped in a situation he didn't choose or want. I truly love his attitude!

His master saw that the Lord was with him and that the Lord caused all that he did to succeed in his hands. So Joseph found favor in his sight and attended him, and he made him overseer of his house and put him in charge of all that he had. From the time that he made him overseer in his house and over all that he had, the Lord blessed the Egyptian's house for Joseph's sake; the blessing of the Lord was on all that he had, in house and field. So he left all that he had in Joseph's charge, and because of him he had no concern about anything but the food he ate. Now Joseph was handsome in form and appearance. Gen. 39:3-6

I remember studying the life of Joseph as a teenager and it had such an impact on the way I viewed the circumstances in my life. We see in Joseph the attitude "How can I serve you here, God?" even in the most difficult times. I recall being in a job I didn't love and struggling with my attitude. Our Bible teacher at our little Christian school happened to be teaching on Joseph's life. I was so convicted! I remember thinking, if Joseph could have the integrity and diligence to work hard as a slave, hundreds of miles from home, surely I could give one hundred percent waiting tables. I have thought of his life and the tremendous example of his work ethic many, many times in my life.

Do the people around me see the kind of integrity that Joseph's master saw in him? What if we each tackled the hard things in our lives with the same gusto and determination that Joseph did? Do our employers know they can fully trust us to work hard with a great attitude, even when they aren't around? Good questions to ponder! Great lessons from Joseph's life.

What kept Joseph from simply giving up and sinking into despair or getting angry and bitter at the unfair turn of his life? He was only a kid! No one would blame him or be surprised if he gave up. I picture myself in that scenario, and I am pretty sure a major meltdown would have ensued. Surely Joseph must have felt forgotten, forsaken, and hopeless. He didn't have the promises from God's Word like we do today. He didn't even have a scrap of scroll with a few psalms on a piece of papyrus. But do you know what he did have? He had the One thing he needed. The only thing. Remember…

"The Lord was with Joseph…" Genesis 39:2a

He had the holy God of heaven, the Creator of the universe, the Beginning and the End, the Great I Am with him. God was enough. God was *all* he needed. I am ashamed to say that even having many copies of God's precious Word—

in my house, on my phone, and every other possible device—even being surrounded by solid biblical teaching, believing friends, and family, scores of encouraging books, radio stations piping through my car with worship music and preaching...I still find myself wallowing in despair. And I bet I'm not alone in that. How can that even be? God, our great God, is *with us*! Emmanuel, God *with us*! Like Joseph, we are not alone! We have everything we need!

We forget, don't we? As the great hymn writer once wrote, "Prone to wander, Lord I feel it, Prone to leave the God I love." That's us in a nutshell. We claim Christ as our own, yet we often live daily lives as practical atheists, doing, wandering, and coping in our own strength. We are weak and forgetful. But here is the great news. God's power is made perfect in our weakness. And His grace will be sufficient to meet all of our needs (2 Cor. 12:9). He really is enough.

Joseph was soon to find out that God would be enough even in a much worse situation. So things seem to be going pretty well for him in the first few verses of Genesis 39. I know he was still a slave, but he was respected, well liked, and trusted. He was in command of the entire estate, and his master didn't concern himself with anything except feeding himself. Wouldn't that be fun for at least one day, to not worry about anything except what delicious food we are going to consume? That was the master's blessed life because of Joseph.

And then comes trouble. And I mean big trouble in the form of Potiphar's slinky wife. I don't really know that she was slinky, but it's kind of how I picture her...slinking in and out of the rooms looking for Joseph. Now, the Bible makes a point of mentioning that Joseph's mother was beautiful. And unfortunately for him, Joseph must have inherited those good looks. As a matter of fact, the Bible says he was, "handsome in form and appearance," to be exact. Joseph was a real hunk, and Potiphar's wife had taken notice. She began to follow him, trying to seduce him, to lure him to her bedroom. In light of the Egyptian culture, there was nothing surprising about her behavior. It was a wholly immoral society filled with debauchery. She wouldn't let up, hounding him daily. Joseph steadfastly refused. Now, let's keep a few things in mind. Joseph was a normal guy with normal desires. In addition, he was in a stressful, tempting situation, far from home, and outside of his dad's watchful eye. Add to this the idea that a powerful man like Potiphar probably had a very beautiful wife, perhaps young like Joseph. This was temptation with a capital T!

Most likely no one else he knew in Egypt was serving Jehovah, the God of his fathers. No one would care if he slept with his master's wife. She certainly wasn't going to tell! But Joseph steadfastly refused to even be in the same room with her. He was the perfect example of "fleeing youthful lusts" (2 Tim. 2:22). You get the picture that Joseph was always on guard, always on watch for her. And when she would enter the room, he would quickly exit. He repeatedly shut her down. And his response to her proposition was so amazing. He didn't make excuses like, "I don't want to lose my job (or my head!) " or "I don't want to get caught." No, his refusal was solely in his desire to honor the God who was ever with him, who had been faithful to him in every way. Look at his humble and beautiful response to this seductive, immoral woman.

"How then can I do this great wickedness and sin against God." Gen. 39:9

He called it what it was. Sin. Wickedness. How often do we sugarcoat our temptations and make excuses for our behavior? Call it what it is! Sin is sin. And our God is ever with us. If only we would keep the desire to honor him always before us as Joseph did!

Well, I'm sure you know the story now. Potiphar's wife was a woman scorned. She has been denied, refused, and rejected. And she was furious! One day she grew desperate and grabbed Joseph by his coat. This was one aggressive woman!

He slipped right out of that coat and ran for his life. Joseph's behavior shows us such great character, and character is not something you're born with. Character is learned behavior, and Joseph was determined to do nothing to dishonor God.

And this was where his situation went downhill. The master came home, heard his wife's sob story, false accusations, and threw Joseph into prison. Now, not only was he a slave in a foreign land where no one knew him, he was a slave in *prison* in a foreign land where no one knew him. Seems impossible, right? But wait!

> But the Lord was with Joseph and showed him steadfast love and gave him favor in the sight of the keeper of the prison. And the keeper of the prison put Joseph in charge of all the prisoners who were in the prison. Whatever was done there, he was the one who did it. The keeper of the prison paid no attention to anything that was in Joseph's charge, because the Lord was with him. And whatever he did, the Lord made it succeed. Gen. 39:21-23

Amazing! Again, the Lord was with him. He was not alone. And God gave Joseph the strength to maintain that "How can I serve you here, God?" attitude. Four times in this passage we are reminded that the Lord was with Joseph. He was never alone, not for a moment. God had good plans in mind for Joseph's life, for the saving of his chosen people. God was completely and sovereignly in control over all of the happenings and circumstances affecting Joseph, and God is completely and sovereignly in control over all the circumstances that affect us. We are not alone for a moment of it.

We are going to finish studying Joseph's life in our next chapter and see how the rest of his story unfolds. I don't think anyone would argue that Joseph showed unusual character and submission to God's plan. He seemed to understand there was a bigger picture at hand. He truly had a surrendered heart.

However, Joseph is not even the best example of a surrendered heart that Scripture has to offer. While his attitude was remarkable and his tenacity admirable, he was still a flawed human being with a sinful heart like the rest of us. No, the very best example of a heart fully surrendered, humbly submitted to an unthinkably painful plan, is our Lord Jesus.

Jesus: the Perfect Surrendered Heart

Here's the deal: from the time of the Fall, that first sin in the Garden of Eden, there has been a great gulf separating a holy God and sinful man. God is holy, righteous, and pure, and we are lost, desperate sinners in dire need of rescue. And that's precisely why Jesus came. He came to be our rescuer, to go to the cross in willing surrender and sacrifice His sinless life to pay the debt we could never pay on our own. The Bible makes it clear that we are all lost sinners, and we cannot reach a holy God on our own or through our good works.

"For all have sinned and fall short of the glory of God." Rom. 3:23

"We have all become like one who is unclean, and all our righteous deeds are like a polluted garment." Is. 64:6

"As it is written: "None is righteous, no, not one; no one understands; no one seeks for God. All have turned aside; together they have become worthless; no one does good, not even one." Rom. 3:10-12

That's the bad news. Thankfully, there is really great news! God saw the broken mess of mankind, our hearts always turning from Him, and He provided a way of salvation because of His great love for us. Not because we deserve it, not because we are good, only because He loves us! In fact, Romans 5, one of my very favorite hope-filled chapters in Scripture, tells us that even when we were enemies of God, He sent His Son for us because He loves us.

"For while we were still weak, at the right time Christ died for the ungodly. For one will scarcely die for a righteous person—though perhaps for a good person one would dare even to die— but God shows his love for us in that while we were still sinners, Christ died for us." Rom. 5:6-8

"For God so loved the world, that he gave his only Son, that whoever believes in him should not perish but have eternal life." John 3:16

"He saved us, not because of works done by us in righteousness, but according to his own mercy. . ." Titus 3:5

Jesus left His perfect place in heaven where angels, cherubim, and seraphim, worshipped Him day and night. He left His beloved Father and all of His glory, and was born into this dirty sin-filled earth as a helpless infant. He was the God-Man—fully God and fully man. When He was thirty-three years old, after He had healed the sick, raised the dead, and performed many other miracles affirming that He was God, He was nailed to the cross by religious leaders who refused to hear the truth. He willingly went to the cross to pay the price for our sins. Man did not take His life from Him; rather He gave it as a sacrifice, a once-for-all-time payment for mankind's sin. Jesus' blood was shed to wash away our sins.

". . .without the shedding of blood there is no forgiveness of sins." Heb. 9:22

"In him we have redemption through his blood, the forgiveness of our trespasses, according to the riches of his grace." Eph. 1:7

"For even the Son of Man came not to be served but to serve, and to give his life as a ransom for many." Mark 10:45

He came to pay our debt, to be our ransom. This is the most important point I will make in this book. Yes, this is a book about trials and the difficult times we all face. But it is my desire that it be a book of hope and encouragement, a reminder that we are not alone even in the darkest pit of circumstance. And until we each come to a realization that we *need* a Savior, that we are sinners in desperate need of rescue, we *are* alone! We *are* without hope! Jesus *is* our hope. He is our answer, our rescuer and our ONLY way to be cleansed and saved and to have a relationship with a holy God. Jesus Himself said it best in the Gospel of John.

"Jesus said to him, "I am the way, and the truth, and the life.
No one comes to the Father except through me." John 14:6

"And there is salvation in no one else, for there is no other name under heaven given among men by which we must be saved." Acts 4:12

Jesus is the one way, the only way for us to be saved. The first step in having a relationship with the holy God of heaven is realizing and admitting that you are indeed a sinner. You must acknowledge that you cannot reach God on your own or through your own good works. You have to recognize that you need rescuing. Secondly, you must understand the simple facts of the gospel and believe in what Jesus has done for you.

"For I delivered to you as of first importance what I also received: that Christ died for our sins in accordance with the Scriptures, that he was buried, that he was raised on the third day in accordance with the Scriptures." 1 Cor. 15:3-4

Jesus went to the cross, died for your sins and mine, and was buried in a tomb of stone. But He didn't stay there! On the third day after He was buried, He rose again, and is now in heaven, seated at the right hand of His Father. And He loves *you* and desires a relationship with *you*! He wants you to come as you are.

"Come to me, all who labor and are heavy laden, and I will give you rest. Take my yoke upon you, and learn from me, for I am gentle and lowly in heart, and you will find rest for your souls. For my yoke is easy, and my burden is light." Matt. 11:28-30

Before we move on in our study, I have to ask: Do you know Him? Have you come to a point in your life of understanding your need of a Savior? His gift of salvation is for you. He longs for you to come and find rest in Him. It is as simple as believing in your heart and confessing Christ as Lord. In the book of Acts, the Philippian jailer understood his need and asked Paul and Silas sincerely, "What must I do to be saved?" They answered very clearly,

"Believe on the Lord Jesus Christ, and you will be saved..." Acts 16:31

"Because, if you confess with your mouth that Jesus is Lord and believe in your heart that God raised him from the dead, you will be saved. For with the heart one believes and is justified, and with the mouth one confesses and is saved. For the Scripture says, "Everyone who believes in him will not be put to shame." For there is no distinction between Jew and Greek; for the same Lord is Lord of all, bestowing his riches on all who call on him. For "everyone who calls on the name of the Lord will be saved."
Rom. 10:9-13

Friend, call on Him! Repent of your sins, believe in what He has done for you in His death on the cross, and be saved. He will rescue you and wash you white as snow. He knows your heart. Simply pray and give your life to Him. Ask Him to come into your life and save you. He will do it. Remember,

..."everyone who calls on the name of the Lord will be saved." Rom. 10:13

That is the very best news I could share with you. Everything else to follow in this book—every Scripture, biblical example, and story—hinges on having a real relationship with Jesus. He is the only way of salvation, He is the ultimate truth, He is our constant strength, and the one real answer in all our trials. He is the only way to have a truly surrendered heart. A heart willing to suffer with courage and grace, growing in maturity and sanctification through His provision and strength.

GINGER MILLERMON

A Forgiving Heart

"...forgiving each other; as the Lord has forgiven you, so you must also forgive."
Col. 3:13

"To forgive is to set a prisoner free and discover that prisoner was you."
Lewis B. Smedes

I t was a quiet, cold night in February of 1997. Joel and I both were recovering from a raging bout of the stomach flu and had been banned from seeing Jarrott in the NICU until we were better. We were six months into our new normal of hospital living with Jarrott. He had stabilized enough to be transferred to a hospital closer to home after his miraculous turn-around at Children's Hospital in Denver. Now he was only seventy miles from home. Although it was still a distance and inconvenient, our family was together more regularly and we had the blessing of local family and church support.

Since Joel was a pastor, we lived in the parsonage next to our little Bible church. The only downside of that was that our home phone was connected to the church's phone and sometimes rang nonstop. We had turned our home phone off to get some sleep and had left instructions with Jarrott's nurses to call Joel's parents, who lived nearby, if there was an emergency. Remember, this was back in the olden days before the convenience of cell phones. Jarrott was stable and was progressing amazingly, so we were comfortable getting the rest we needed to quickly recover and get back to the hospital.

It was around two in the morning when we heard pounding on our front door and soon the voices of Joel's parents. The hospital had called. Our hearts pounding, we called into the nurse's station in the NICU.

"You guys need to come right away. Jarrott's trach plugged and he was down with no heartbeat for several minutes before we finally resuscitated him. He is having major seizures and we don't know if he is going to make it through the night. You need to come." The news was devastating.

We numbly got dressed and raced to the car. We had seventy miles to wonder if he would still be alive when we arrived. Joel got pulled over part way into our trip and was going so fast the officer threatened to throw him in jail. We pleaded with him to let us continue so we could get to Jarrott. He mercifully let us go with an admonition to slow down. He reminded us we would do our son no good if we didn't arrive safely. The trip took forever.

We finally arrived and were ushered quickly into Jarrott's room. The site that met us shook us to the core. He was sedated and unconscious, with tremors shaking his little body. The medical staff tearfully shared that he had a major brain insult. He had literally been dead with no heartbeat for an undetermined amount of time and he was very unstable. Jarrott was in an isolation room by himself and somehow his equipment that monitored his heart and oxygen saturation levels had not alarmed at the nurses' station. By the time they discovered there was an emergency, he was already blue and had flatlined. It took them more than five minutes to revive him.

It quickly became apparent to us that human error had allowed major time to pass before anyone noticed Jarrott was in distress. We never got a clear picture or answer about what happened that night. It was especially heartbreaking because we had already been through so much, he had suffered and beat incredible odds, and was finally making huge strides. His milestones and progress in recent weeks had greatly encouraged us, and we understood that this was a life changing, perhaps fatal, setback. The damage this episode would most likely inflict upon his brain would be irreparable. His doctor's sadly gave us a very grim prognosis.

At this point, Joel and I realized we were faced with a choice. Yes, we were angry. I will not sugarcoat the emotions that flooded us. Anger, grief, and questions threatened to overwhelm us. But we knew Jarrott's doctors and nurses loved him with a passion. They had been tireless in their care of him and were advocates every single day for him. Unlike our experience at our previous hospital where we were encouraged to let him die, this hospital staff was constantly cheering him on and fighting for him.

Over the following days as the tremors slowly faded and we settled into another "new" normal, unsure what to expect, Joel and I both fought against the anger and bitterness we knew would bring nothing good. We acknowledged that a mistake was made by good people who loved and cared for our son. Mistakes happen. We had the choice to be consumed and eaten up with anger and to assign blame...or we could forgive.

Forgiveness is never the easy choice. We naturally want to hang onto our grievances and make others pay for their mistakes. Joel and I separately had to make the conscious decision to forgive...even in those moments we didn't feel the forgiveness. And some days we chose better than others— forgiveness is often a daily battle. We had to choose to forgive and trust that even in this new, difficult turn of events, God had a good plan. Jarrott's tragic episode did not take a sovereign God by surprise. He was there. He knew.

Maybe you have not faced deep and painful tragedy per se, but we have each suffered our own hurts, betrayals, and crushing events…often at the hand of another person. What is our response? Where do we go with that? Forgiveness can be such a huge issue and obstacle in our walk with Christ. We have already seen in two instances from Scripture how destructive it can be to hold on to grudges and anger. The ripple effect of unforgiveness can go on and on.

As we consider the lives of Cain and Joseph in our last chapter, we understand we get to choose. We get to choose our attitude; we choose anger, hatred, and bitterness…or forgiveness.

I will never forget as a young girl hearing the story of Corrie Ten Boom. I read her book, *The Hiding Place*, and it affected me deeply, specifically concerning the issue of forgiveness. Corrie and her family were part of the Dutch Resistance hiding Jews and underground workers during the Holocaust. Knowing the consequences should they be caught, the family built a false wall in Corrie's room and hid up to seven Jews at a time. It is estimated they saved 800 Jewish lives. In February of 1944 the Gestapo raided the Ten Boom's home, and they were arrested and sent to concentration camps. Their elderly father only lasted a few days before he died. Over ten months Corrie and her sister, Betsie, were transferred to three different prisons, and within a year, Betsie died in Ravensbrück Camp. However Corrie was mistakenly released due to a clerical error, and a few days later all of the women her age were killed. God obviously had plans for Corrie Ten Boom! At age 53, she began a worldwide ministry testifying to God's love and speaking on forgiveness.

God will give us the love to be able to forgive our enemies—Corrie Ten Boom

Those were words Corrie lived by and shared for years. Never was her resolve to forgive so tested as at one church service in Munich in 1947. She had finished speaking, sharing her story and message of forgiveness, when a prison guard from Ravensbrück approached her. She instantly recognized

him, though he obviously had no recollection of her specifically. There had been thousands of women in the camp. He
thrust his hand out to her and asked for her forgiveness for
the atrocities he had been a part of in that unspeakable concentration camp. He had come to Christ and knew that God
had forgiven him, but he wanted to personally ask for Corrie's forgiveness. Realizing there was no power within her to
forgive him, in faith and obedience she put her hand into his.
She understood that forgiveness is a choice. It is not an emotion, it is an act of obedience and will. She chose to stretch
out her arm and place her hand into his, trusting God to help
her truly forgive. And He did. As their hands clasped together God filled her heart with incredible forgiveness, and she
was able to utter those beautiful words, "I forgive you!" She
chose obedience, and God provided the emotion and a heart
filled with love.

This beautiful story convicts my heart on the little things
I tend to hang on to instead of forgive. How often do we tell
someone we forgive them but every chance we get, we throw
their mistakes back in their face? We say the words, "I forgive you," but we never really let it go and move on. Proverbs
sums it up here:

> "Whoever covers an offense seeks love,
> but he who repeats a matter separates close friends." Prov.17:9

We must be willing to forgive and let it go, to choose to
"cover an offense" as Proverbs says. Often the circumstances
and trials we find ourselves in are not a result of our own sin
or a result of a natural happening or illness. Sometimes they
are the result of someone else's sin. We are wronged, shat-
tered by perhaps even someone we love, and we struggle to
forgive.

Let's go back to Genesis to the continuing story of Joseph
and his willingness to "cover" his brother's sins. In Genesis
39, we left off with Joseph in prison. How alone he must have

felt! But God was with him, watching over him, and miraculously had him released from prison. Joseph was seventeen when he was sold into slavery, and he was thirty when he was released from prison. Thirteen years have passed when we pick up our story. Joseph had spent several years in prison and had been released to interpret Pharaoh's dreams and was made second in command over all of Egypt. God had divinely appointed Joseph to be in this position. Joseph was put in charge of all the food in the land, as a great famine loomed on the horizon. Pharaoh's dreams indicated that there would be seven years of plenty followed by seven years of severe famine. Joseph began to store up massive amounts of food in various cities—food that would be used and distributed during the lean years of famine. Not much is said in Scripture about Joseph during this season of his life. He was given a wife, had two sons and was "fruitful in the land of my affliction," as he was quoted to say in Genesis 41:52. But the seven years of plenty has to end, and he was thirty-seven years old when the famine hit. The famine was widespread, "in all lands," (Gen. 41:54) except the land of Egypt. There was bread there because the storehouses were full, thanks to Joseph's wisdom, management, and planning. All of Egypt swarmed to Joseph for food. And not only Egypt. Soon the whole earth came to Joseph to buy grain, including his evil, manipulative, murderous brothers.

While Joseph sat in that dirty prison cell, a few years earlier, there was no way he could have imagined how circumstances would unfold in his life. I wonder if Joseph had sat bitterly in that cell, angry, hateful, and perhaps even scheming revenge toward his brothers, would he have been in a position to be so greatly used by God? He could have had no inkling of the future God had planned for him. It is a good lesson to me to remember that when my circumstances are dire, unpleasant, or seem impossible, I have no idea what God has planned! Instead of stewing, planning revenge, or having a giant pity party, Joseph was simply faithful. That is the perfect word to sum up his life. Faithful.

So Genesis Chapter 42 opens with Joseph's family suffering and starving, hundreds of miles away. The whole earth, everyone who wanted to eat, had to go to Egypt for food. So down to Egypt traveled the sons of Jacob, Joseph's ten brothers. Except Benjamin, Joseph's only full brother, was left behind. Benjamin was the only other child born to Jacob by his beloved wife, Rachel, whom he lost in childbirth when Benjamin was born. Jacob was unwilling to part with this youngest son after the disappearance of Joseph twenty years earlier.

The scene unfolds with Joseph being governor of the land and the one who sold all the grain to the people. When Joseph's brothers arrived seeking food, they had no idea they were bowing before their brother, the one they had abused and treated so inhumanely. Joseph was clean-shaven like an Egyptian instead of having a beard like the Hebrews wore, and though he understood and spoke Hebrew, he posed as an Egyptian and used an interpreter. I wonder what Joseph was thinking when he saw them there, twenty years later? Some commentators think he must have been watching for them, knowing they would have to come for food. His last interaction with his brothers was crying out to them in terror, begging for his life as they sold him into slavery. He could probably remember every detail of the hatred and scorn on their faces, blurred through his tears as he pleaded with them.

Now, as his brothers bowed before him, Joseph immediately remembered the dreams he had as a teenager. The dreams his brothers hated! He saw the literal fulfillment of those dreams before his very eyes! Joseph managed to stay calm and collected, keeping his identity hidden, and began to test them to see if they had changed their wicked ways. He wanted to know specifically about his brother Benjamin. I'm sure he had always wondered if they had been as cruel to his younger brother as they had been to him.

Joseph began a time of testing, and accused his brothers of being spies and threw them in jail for three days. When they were brought back before Joseph, they began to argue amongst themselves. In fact, as he sat listening to his brother's argue in Hebrew, he heard their confession and guilt for what they had done to him. They *knew* they were being punished for what they'd done to Joseph.

"Then they said to one another, 'In truth we are guilty concerning our brother, in that we saw the distress of his soul, when he begged us and we did not listen. That is why this distress has come upon us.'" Gen. 42:21

Their guilt was hitting them full force. It was too much for Joseph to hear and he excused himself and went to another room to weep. When he composed himself and returned, he had made a decision. He told the brothers that one of them would have to stay. He had Simeon tied up right before their eyes and taken away to jail. He ordered them not to return to Egypt for food unless they brought their youngest brother with them. Joseph knew the famine was not nearly over, and they would have to return if they were going to survive. He wanted to see his beloved brother, Benjamin, with his own eyes. And he wasn't finished testing the integrity of his brothers. Had they changed? Would they sell out Benjamin, their father's second favorite son, as they had Joseph? He was determined to find out.

The men returned home with their tails between their legs. Not only was Simeon in prison, but when they ran out of food again, they had to return with Benjamin, and they knew it would kill their father. As their food dwindled, Jacob held out as long as possible, refusing to allow Benjamin to go with them. I find it interesting that no one really mentions the fact that Simeon is rotting in jail in Egypt. Months pass by as Simeon sits in prison, probably wondering if they will ever come back for him. He certainly had plenty of time to think about what had possibly happened to his brother Joseph when they had betrayed him.

The food in Jacob's family finally ran out. The brothers

were not anxious to return to Egypt and go before the harsh ruler, and their father was anguished to think of sending Benjamin, but there was no choice. Back to Egypt they traveled, dreading what was to come, terrified of something happening to their father's precious Benjamin.

When Joseph finally laid eyes on his little brother, he again had to excuse himself, going into his own chambers to weep. How he had longed for this day! He never thought he would see his beloved brother again. But he couldn't reveal his identity yet! There was one more important thing he had to know. Would his brothers look for the chance to betray Benjamin? He had heard the anguish in their voices when they recalled what they had done to Joseph. Had there been true change and repentance? Joseph was about to find out.

After releasing Simeon from prison and having the men come to his home for lunch, which basically scared them to death, Joseph had their bags filled with grain and sent them on their way. Unbeknownst to them, he had placed his special silver cup in Benjamin's bag. The real test was about to begin. He allowed the men get out of the city a short distance and down the road. They must have been heaving a *huge* sigh of relief! They were all on their way home! Simeon had been released from prison, and Benjamin was safe. Jacob would be so pleased, so relieved. They had promised their father they would return Benjamin to him, and they were on the homestretch!

But, wait! What was that in the distance? Riders came upon them, Joseph's stewards pulled up alongside them and halted their progress. The steward accused them of stealing Joseph's special cup and demanded to look in their bags. The men were flabbergasted! They insisted they were innocent and quickly and willingly lowered their bags, even going so far as to proclaim if the stolen cup was found, the thief should die, and the rest of them would return as servants. They *knew* that cup wouldn't be found in their grain. They had no idea they had been set up.

I can almost hear the wail of disbelief and horror as Benjamin's sack was opened and the cup lifted out. The men tore their clothes in anguish. They were so close to accomplishing their mission! How had that silver cup gotten in Benjamin's bag? They solemnly mounted their donkeys and headed back to Egypt, their stomachs soured with dread. Now this is where this ancient account turns so incredibly dramatic and beautiful.

Joseph had set this scenario up perfectly for his brothers to rid themselves of another favorite child. This was their chance. The cup was found in Benjamin's bag…Benjamin would pay the price. The brothers could have simply left Benjamin there and headed home, rid of another problem. Joseph needed to know their disposition toward Benjamin. I'm not sure if their response was what he expected, but I'm sure he couldn't have been more pleased and relieved. The men fell on their faces before Joseph. They offered themselves all as slaves. Joseph very reasonably insisted only Benjamin would be a slave, the rest could return home to their father. And this was where Judah stepped up to offer his life for Benjamin. Judah, who had been the one to hatch the grand plan to sell Joseph. Judah, who didn't bat an eye while Joseph begged for mercy. Judah, who previously had no compassion on the grief he would bring to his father by pretending a wild animal had torn apart Joseph. This same Judah begged Joseph to let him take Benjamin's place because it would kill their father if Benjamin didn't return. Judah had grown into a man of character and integrity. Joseph's brothers passed his test with flying colors. And now it was time for the big reveal.

Joseph had seen all he needed to see, and he could hide his emotions no longer. He sent his servants and everyone from the room except for his brothers. Those eleven men must have been genuinely confused! Joseph was weeping so loudly that the whole household of Pharaoh could hear him. Through his tears Joseph finally made himself known.

"And Joseph said to his brothers, 'I am Joseph! Is my father still alive?'
But his brothers could not answer him, for they were dismayed at his presence."
Gen. 45:3

I don't think there was anything that could have shocked those brothers more! Joseph was alive? Joseph was in charge of Egypt? Their shock quickly turned to fear. Dismayed is not a strong enough word...terrified would be more accurate. If they were afraid of this man before, they had every reason to be petrified now! The brother they betrayed nearly twenty-five years earlier was now in control of their fate. He held their lives in his hands. Surely he would seek revenge! And here's where Joseph continued to model an incredible, forgiving heart. He drew them near to himself, still weeping, and offered them these sweet, reassuring words.

"...I am your brother Joseph, whom you sold into Egypt. And now do not be distressed or angry with yourselves because you sold me here, for God sent me before you to preserve life. For the famine has been in the land these two years, and there are yet five years in which there will be neither plowing nor harvest. And God sent me before you to preserve for you a remnant on earth, and to keep alive for you many survivors. So it was not you who sent me here, but God." Gen. 45:4-8

Think back with me for a moment over the past twenty-plus years of Joseph's life. From enduring scorn and hatred at the hands of his brothers, the heartbreak of being torn from his family, to being a slave of Potiphar, falsely accused by a scorned woman, hopelessly languishing in prison as a slave... Joseph had endured unthinkable trials, all as a direct result of his brothers. He had lost decades of his life when he could have been enjoying his family and father. He had every human reason to be angry and bitter at his brothers. Every right from a human standpoint to hate them and seek revenge. And oh! This was the perfect opportunity for revenge! All of the cards were in Joseph's hands. He controlled their very lives, and they knew it. I'm sure they were trembling in fear.

I don't know about you, but I know myself, and I'm quite convinced my response would not have been so gracious and kind. Joseph continued in a tender speech to his long-lost brothers, reassuring them that he had a plan to save them already in place. He told them to hurry back home and return with their father and their families. He would provide for them, even giving them the best land in Egypt for their flocks. There was nothing he hadn't thought of in his provision for them. He concluded his speech by falling on their necks, weeping and kissing them, holding them tightly. Honestly, it brings tears to my eyes to think of the overwhelming joy he must have felt after so many years apart from his family. Finally holding them close, reunited at last. Joseph convinced his brothers to go get their father and families, and soon he had an emotional reunion with his dad. I can't imagine the joy for both of them.

I love the very end of this story, seeing Joseph's heart one last time. In Genesis 50, Jacob is already an old man at 130 years old. God gives him another seventeen years to enjoy with his newfound son, and at age 147, Jacob breathed his last breath. This is where it is interesting to me. Even after all those years, Joseph's brothers still wondered if he would take revenge on them.

"When Joseph's brothers saw that their father was dead, they said, 'It may be that Joseph will hate us and pay us back for all the evil that we did to him.' So they sent a message to Joseph, saying, 'Your father gave this command before he died: 'say to Joseph, "Please forgive the transgression of your brothers and their sin, because they did evil to you."' And now, please forgive the transgression of the servants of the God of your father.' Joseph wept when they spoke to him." Gen. 50:15-17

Their dad had died and those men thought they were toast! Surely Joseph was so kind to them simply to impress their father. And now that Jacob was gone…they were going to pay the price for their long ago sins. Joseph's response was so very beautiful. He wept because it had not even occurred to him to take revenge. Instead he comforted them with re-assuring words.

> "But Joseph said to them, 'Do not fear, for am I in the place of God? As for you, you meant evil against me, but God meant it for good, to bring it about that many people should be kept alive, as they are today. So do not fear; I will provide for you and your little ones.' Thus he comforted them and spoke kindly to them." Gen. 50:19-21

Do you think if Joseph had kept bitterness stewing and brewing in his heart all those years that he would have been able to respond with such grace and mercy at this moment? Do you suppose if he had held on to the sins and betrayal of his brothers that he could have seen that God had a bigger picture in mind? Joseph's focus through his life, even as a teenager, had been to honor his God. He had been rejected, betrayed, sold, enslaved, accused, imprisoned, and seemingly forgotten. Yet even in the worst circumstances, he surrendered his heart and unfair circumstances and walked in obedience. And that included forgiveness. What an amazing model he is to us.

I venture to say most of us have not been through anything remotely close to Joseph's painful life. We have all probably felt the sting of rejection, the heartache of betrayal, the misery of being falsely accused, the hopelessness of feeling forgotten. And we have a choice. Will we wallow in self-pity? Will we immerse ourselves in the mire of unforgiveness and cling to bitterness as it sinks its claws into our souls? What is our response to the grievous things in life that befall us, specifically at the hand of others, whether intentionally meaning to hurt us or not?

I have talked to many, many people who sit in the church pew every Sunday whose stubborn refusal to let go of past hurts is astounding. They cannot see that unforgiveness taints every aspect of their walk with Christ and hinders their growth, joy, and peace. We forget as we hang on to past offenses that unforgiveness rots into bitterness and becomes an emotional cancer that eats away at our souls. I heard an old saying once that had an impact on me: "Unforgiveness is like drinking poison and expecting the other person to die." How true.

I will never forget a pastor friend telling us many years ago that one of his elders was suing him, both of the men still active in the same church. What? How can these things be within our churches, within our hearts? We are instructed clearly in God's Word to forgive. The command to forgive is… a command. It is not an optional emotion or attitude. It is a call to obedience by our Father who loves us and knows what is best for us.

"…forgiving each other; as the Lord has forgiven you, so you must also forgive."
Col. 3:13

We must forgive. When I think of Joseph and his amazing, forgiving heart, I am reminded of the obvious parallels to the One who is perfect at forgiving.

Jesus: the Perfect Forgiving Heart

The teaching of the rabbis during Jesus' day would encourage people to forgive those who offended them…but only up to three times. Three times. Were these people never married?

"Oops, honey, you ticked me off three times now! You're out of here!" I guess maybe that went right along with their leniency to divorce over almost anything. It seems like most people would only be married about a week if it was "three strikes you're out." I love that Peter came to Jesus to ask Him some questions about forgiveness, and Peter threw out a new number. One he probably felt was *quite* generous.

"Peter came up and said to him, 'Lord, how often will my brother sin against me, and I forgive him? As many as seven times?' Jesus said to him, "I do not say to you seven times, but seventy-seven times.'" Matt.18: 21-22

Many versions say "seventy times seven." That's four hundred and ninety times…but I don't think the number of times was Jesus' point. The point was this: we should quit counting and simply forgive, over and over and over and over again.

Jesus went on in His conversation with Peter and shared a parable we should all heed. He told about a king who was settling the accounts of his servants. There were serious consequences for those servants who wouldn't or couldn't pay their debts. There really weren't too many payment plans going on in biblical times. If a person couldn't pay their debts, the lender could seize the borrower and his family and force them to work until the debt was repaid. Or the debtor could be thrown into prison indefinitely, until someone, somehow paid what was owed. Slavery, prison, or even torture awaited those who didn't pay their loans. That is the background of our story.

So a king was looking at his accounts and realized one of his servants owed him a massive amount of money. We are talking millions upon millions of dollars. A ridiculous, impossible amount. Jesus was telling this story, and was making a point to use a giant sum of money. When the servant couldn't pay it back, the king ordered him and his wife and children to be sold as slaves and all their property sold. Wow! Harsh times! The man fell to his knees and begged for more time. He begged for the king to be patient and he would pay it back. I don't know how he thought he would pay back millions, but he must have been pretty convincing because the king was moved with pity and forgave him the debt. Forgave the debt! Millions! His slate was wiped clean, and he was released a free man. Amazing!

Can you imagine his exhilaration, as he must have raced from the king's presence, not giving him any time to change his mind? His heart pounding, his chest heaving, he had to get home and share the incredible news with his wife! Debt canceled! Free! He was free! They were all free!

And then…out of the corner of his eye, who did he see but a man who owed him money. Not a lot of money, only a little amount. About a large pizza's worth or something trivial like that. So what was his reaction going to be? Obviously he was going to share his great news and cancel that man's teeny tiny debt, right? Nope. Didn't happen. That man, who had been given his life back, spared a destiny of slavery, grabbed the poor servant who owed him about twenty bucks and started to strangle him in rage. "Pay me what you owe!" he demanded cruelly. That second servant begged now for his life. "Give me a little bit more time! Be patient with me and I will pay you!" Sound familiar? But the wicked, ungrateful servant could not be swayed to forgive that small debt.

Well, when the other servants got wind of what was going on, they were "greatly distressed." They rushed back to the king and told him what had taken place. The king was enraged! The unforgiving servant was brought back before the king.

"'You wicked servant! I forgave you all that debt because you pleaded with me. And should not you have had mercy on your fellow servant, as I had mercy on you?' And in anger his master delivered him to the jailers, until he should pay all his debt."
Matt. 18:32-34

Now, honestly, my sinful, self-righteous little heart feels pretty good about the end of this story! That ungrateful servant makes me so mad! How could he do that? How could he not forgive that insignificant debt when his life was handed back to him? He deserved to go to prison!

And then I read the next verse…

"So also my heavenly Father will do to every one of you, if you do not forgive your brother from your heart." Matt. 18:35

Ouch. Instantly my mind is flooded with all the things

that I want to hold on to and refuse to forgive. Here's the thing: we have been forgiven the millions. Beyond millions. A debt innumerable, insurmountable, and immeasurable by any human standard. We have been redeemed, given life! Rescued from an eternal destiny of suffering in hell. Since Jesus paid our debt on the cross, now we can come to him for cleansing, healing, and forgiveness, and our debt is wiped clean. The penalty we owe for our sins before a holy God is gone! Jesus paid it *all*! It is finished! It is done! It is over! Washed clean, forgiven, cleansed, and set free! The old is gone, the new has come. We have new life in Christ. Let that sink in for one glorious second.

And then ask yourself: how in the world can we not forgive each other? How can we have our impossible debt, sin, and guilt wiped clean and not be willing to forgive our brother or sister? Why do we hang on to things, sometimes even little offenses from our childhood, and refuse to move on? I am preaching to myself today. We cannot withhold forgiveness from others. We have to adopt a generous, merciful attitude of forgiveness. I know it's hard, it's a battle every day. I have my "issues" I want to grasp on to and hide away in my heart. I'll forgive everything except…that. That's not how Christ forgives us. He forgives *all*. And we are clearly called in His Word to forgive.

Jesus' own words in John 15 say,

"If you love me, you will keep my commandments."

And His command is to forgive:

"Be kind to one another, tenderhearted, forgiving one another, as God in Christ forgave you." Eph. 4:32

I'm so glad God doesn't forgive our sins the way we forgive each other: slowly, reluctantly, and grudgingly. Oh no! He forgives fully, tenderly, generously, and lovingly. Praise

God, we have been forgiven! Now in deep love and gratitude to our precious Savior who gave all, who shed His blood on the tree, willingly giving His life as our ransom, *we* love, *we* are kind, and *we* forgive.

I am certain that many of you reading this book are dealing with unbelievable pain, hurt, and scars inflicted by others. What are you doing with that pain? How are you coping? Are you bitter? Have you forgiven? Let us embrace God's Word on this issue. Let us, by the example of Christ and in obedience to His Word, have a forgiving heart.

"...forgiving each other; as the Lord has forgiven you, so you must also forgive."
Col. 3:13

CHAPTER FOUR

A Thankful Heart

"Giving thanks always and for everything to God the Father
in the name of our Lord Jesus Christ."
Ephesians 5:20

"Giving thanks to God for both His temporal and spiritual blessings in our lives
is not just a nice thing to do - it is the moral will of God.
Failure to give Him the thanks due Him is sin."
Jerry Bridges

It's not a natural thing to be thankful in the midst of trials. It is rarely our first emotion, and often, when we are suffering, we shove any gratefulness we might have to the back of our minds. Our focus shifts solely to our trial, and we can't seem to see beyond our immediate circumstances. Most of us probably know we are supposed to be thankful in all things, but practically speaking, we forget pretty quickly when trouble comes to visit.

Several years ago, Joel and I were on a short tour to the beautiful Northwest, through Portland, Puget Sound, and Seattle. We had recently adopted our daughter and had been through several months of significant financial strain, and we were incredibly blessed that particular weekend. We had packed in several concerts and women's conferences, CD sales had been very good, and we were both so grateful. Maybe you have been there, under the strain and burden of trying to make ends meet with four kids. We were in the thick of it! As we prepared to head home, it seemed like that financial burden had rolled off a bit and we could breathe a little easier. I remember distinctly being in our rental car, thanking the Lord for His abundant and bountiful provision to meet our needs. We were overwhelmed with His goodness.

A few hours after that sweet thanksgiving service in our car, we were robbed. We still aren't sure how it happened, but the most important bag that carried all of our expensive sound equipment and our moneybag, was stolen right from under our noses. Our computer and media program that ran our entire ministry, our microphones, in-ear monitors, everything we had profited that week, and much more were simply gone. Thousands of dollars in equipment and cash. To say we were crushed is a vast understatement. The news got worse as the day wore on and we found out our insurance would only replace our computer. The rest was considered business and not personal content and was not covered by our insurance. It was almost a total loss.

I have to say, I have never been more impressed by my husband than I was that day. Angry? Yes. Frustrated, disappointed, sucker-punched, and overwhelmed? Yes. Defeated and ready to throw in the towel? Nope. Not a chance. After making the police report, we had a four-hour drive to the airport to fly back home. He spent that entire time ordering new equipment and placing calls to make sure we would have everything we needed to be ready to go for our upcoming conference in New York only four days later. I would like to stop the story here and let you assume we both handled the experience so calmly and with such grace.

But I won't...because we didn't. Well, to be clear, I didn't. While Joel was making the police report, I was making calls to our parents and a few close friends. I felt defeated, and more than ready to quit. I had been privately struggling with discouragement in the previous months and was already wondering if it was time for us to move on from this ministry before this even happened. This incident sealed the deal for me. I *knew* there was absolutely no way we could recover from a loss like this since we were barely making ends meet.

As I was panicking over our situation, I called my dear friend and pastor's wife. I will never forget her response to me after I tearfully shared the whole mess. She was quiet for a moment then asked softly,

"So…have you seen how God is going to use this in your life yet?"

Wait. What? Was she serious? Did she not realize how terrible this was? Should I have been clearer? I don't remember my exact response, but I'm pretty sure it was not super positive.

She continued excitedly. "I can't *wait* to see what God is going to do now!"

Somewhere in the middle of this conversation, I remembered that I had spent that week speaking to women about trials…specifically how to trust God and be at peace in our trials. I had spent hours teaching how to be thankful in trials and that we should have joy and contentment no matter what happens in our lives. It's easy to say the words and preach the sermon, isn't it? It's so much harder to live it out in difficult circumstances.

My friend's kind, honest words were a wakeup call to me. God gently reminded me of His faithfulness and goodness, and we continued to step forward in faith. And do you know what? God did show us amazing things through that robbery!

As word spread about our loss, several individuals and even a Christian school where we had ministered called to ask if they could donate toward our equipment. God provided all that we needed and more. As I mentioned, we were due in New York the very next weekend after the theft. We were doing a Bible conference with Woodrow Kroll and I had always loved listening to him on the radio so it was an honor to minister with him. When he heard what we had been through the previous weekend, he enthusiastically encouraged all the conferees to take my music home. We literally stepped back and watched in amazement as God provided through CD and book sales. He faithfully restored what we had lost with newer and better equipment we could never have afforded. And for me personally, I had a renewed peace that we were doing exactly what He had called us to do.

Through His patience and faithfulness in what seemed to be an insurmountable loss, He proved again that He is worthy of our trust. And at the end of the day, we were overwhelmed with gratefulness for the lessons we had learned. I shamefully confessed my initial panic and distrust, and I continue to be so thankful for His patience with me when I forget. And I do forget…more than I'd like to admit.

It's often so hard to see the big picture, isn't it? We see only our immediate circumstances and can't imagine how God could work them out or redeem them. I look back to when we lived in beautiful Paonia, Colorado. The little town called the "Fruit Capital of the Northfork" is nestled in a valley of orchards, surrounded by majestic mountains and mesas. It is stunning! Occasionally while we lived there, we would go mountain climbing, and it was amazing and exhila-rating to stand on the peak of a 12,000-foot mountain feeling like we were on top of the world! It was always so crisply in-vigorating at the top. However, I realized something up there while observing the glorious view: nothing is growing on the mountaintop. There are only vast fields of barren, dry shale. Oxygen is thin. There's no soil, only layer after layer of rock. But as I looked toward the valley floor far, far below, I noted the green trees, the lush vegetation, the orchards…and the fruit. What a reminder! We want that adrenaline boosting, mountaintop experience, to see the whole horizon, the big picture all the time. But our fruit most often grows in the depths and shadows of the dark valleys. We want predict-able lives, smooth sailing, but how will we ever grow if we don't face adversity and see the provision and goodness of God? We can hear stories of God's faithfulness to others, but until *we* experience His faithfulness, provision, and peace, it doesn't become personal and real to us.

Living in Kansas, I love the predictability of cruising down a long stretch of flat highway. Sometimes in western parts of the state, you're lucky if you even spot a tree or perhaps a grazing deer. It's you and the road and the wide-open sky. You can see ahead for miles upon miles. I really like my life to be like that—no bends in the road to wonder about, no valleys to forge, rivers to swim, or mountains to cross. Smooth, easy, and predictable. Well, for one, that's not realistic at all. Remember back to the Fall in the garden? Life is going to be hard...it's the curse. And secondly, God usually has different plans than that gentle, easy trail. I heard someone once say, "We want simple trails but God likes to go off-road." What a perfect word picture! We want to be cruising down the Kansas 1-70 of life and God wants to take us four-wheeling in the Rocky Mountains over the Continental Divide...because we have to trust Him, lean on Him, and rely on His guidance. The responsibility that we have as we forge through those valleys and over those mountains is that we are grateful to God, knowing that He has good plans ahead for us. We don't have to see the big picture, and we don't have to know what lies ahead.

Do you want to know what God's will for you is today as you face the trials that loom in front of you? Well, I'm glad you asked! Listen to what the apostle Paul said about God's will for us in trials.

"Rejoice always, pray without ceasing, give thanks in all circumstances; for this is the will of God in Christ Jesus for you." 1 Thess. 5:16-18

I would say Paul's words are perfectly clear. Are you in a trial? Then rejoice, pray, and be thankful. That is God's perfect plan and desire for each of us as we face adversity. It's easier said than done, I know. But Paul is the perfect person to give us these words of exhortation. He knew about trials. He wasn't writing from the comfort of his living room, sitting on the couch in front of a cozy fire, and neatly penning letters to the churches. He was constantly on the move, traveling from church to church, city to city to share the gospel, often only one step ahead of those who wanted him dead. He was a wanted, hunted man! He had faced incredible obstacles, life-threatening circumstances, and overwhelming physical hardships. In fact, in 2 Corinthians 11:24 he lists several of the unbelievable things he had suffered. You almost get a sense that he is listing quickly, off the top of his head, a few of his horrific trials. Countless beatings, five separate times receiving the thirty-nine lashes from the Jews, three ship-wrecks, a stoning, danger in every possible situation, sleep-less, cold hungry nights, often near death…the list goes on.

How did he even survive all of that? He had such in-credible perseverance and focus to push ahead and spread the good news no matter the cost! In addition to all of the physical pain he endured, his greatest pain and sorrow was the burden and anxiety he carried for the believers, his "chil-dren." Despite all of that, he kept pushing forward. In fact, you can see his heart in his own words to the Ephesian elders before he goes to Jerusalem and is arrested, in Acts 20:24.

"But I do not account my life of any value nor as precious to myself, if only I may finish my course and the ministry that I received from the Lord Jesus, to testify to the gospel of the grace of God." Act 20:24

The only thing of value to Paul was the gospel. His big-gest desire was to run the race faithfully and finish the course and ministry that God had entrusted to him. Paul beautiful-ly exemplified a thankful heart, content with whatever God brought along his path, whether times of ease or of tragedy. In every one of Paul's letters, with the exception of Galatians, he began with words of thanksgiving. Isn't that amazing? I think that's so significant considering the life of hardship he lived. He had a thankful heart and encouraged his readers, and us, that it is certainly God's desire for us to be thankful in all things. It's very interesting to note that in Romans 1, when Paul is describing the downward spiral of mankind, before he lists all of the perversions that are rampant both in his time and now in our culture, he tells the Romans that man "...did not honor Him as God or give thanks to Him..."

He says something similar in 2 Timothy as he warns of the last days and the attitudes that will prevail then. Among being lovers of self and money, proud, arrogant, heartless, treacherous, and more, Paul says men will be ungrateful. Unthankful. This should give us pause. Ungratefulness is listed with heinous sins we would never want to be accused of committing. And yet we are often discontent with our circumstances and our possessions. We are commanded, as children of the Most High and Holy God, to be a grateful people. We are to shift our focus from the immediate and lift thankful hearts to our trustworthy God.

I recently revisited the account of the lepers from Luke 17 and was reminded of the importance of giving thanks. Jesus was on His way to Jerusalem and was passing through Samaria and Galilee. Right before entering a village, he heard the voices of ten lepers crying out to Him. These men were shunned from their community and family, left to fend for themselves outside the city gate. They were unclean, unwanted, and destitute. Their situation was hopeless. And then they heard that Jesus was coming! They knew the stories, had heard of His amazing miracles, and they obviously hoped Jesus would heal them. They weren't going to let that opportunity pass! They yelled to him, desperate to get his attention. "Jesus, Master, have mercy on us."

Jesus had such compassion on them. He stopped and addressed them in His great mercy and told them to go show themselves to the priests. He was letting them know He would heal them. Once they proved that they were cleansed, they could resume their life within the city walls with their families. So they went on their way, and as they walked, their leprosy disappeared! They were completely clean! Can you imagine their conversation as they ran to the temple?

"Hey, your nose is back!" Or "Look! My fingers are healed! My arms are clear! I've got ten toes again!" What excitement! What relief! Healing meant new life to these ten men. It was freedom from a death sentence. They ran with joy to show the priests!

And then one man, one solitary man, in his overwhelming relief at being granted a new beginning, stopped cold in his race to the priests. I imagine tears streamed down his filthy cheeks as he turned on that dusty road and sprinted back to Jesus, throwing himself at His feet. With a voice louder than the one that had cried for pity and healing, he offered his exuberant praise to God, facedown at Jesus' feet in thankfulness.

Jesus looked up from this man prostrate at His feet and asked simply, "Were not ten cleansed? Where are the nine?" Unbelievably, once the other lepers were healed, they gave no thought to the Healer! Only one man, and a Samaritan at that, returned to give thanks and to show his genuine faith with a grateful heart.

While it's easy to throw stones at the ungrateful nine who went on their way, I have to honestly look in my own heart and wonder, "How often is that me?" How often do I beg and plead at Jesus feet for the thing that is breaking my heart, for my desperate need, but when He answers I just keep moving forward in relief without stopping to thank Him? What would it look like if we thanked Him as much as we asked Him? Instead we often have an attitude of entitlement, feeling as if we deserve our prayers to be answered on *our* timetable, and we completely forget that God's ways and plans are so much higher than ours (Is. 55:8). He sees and knows that big picture. Oh, that my heart would be like that precious, thankful leper...immediately recognizing the sweet answers to prayer and quick to give Him thanks!

I wish all of our prayers were answered that quickly, that clearly, definitely, and immediately. But they are not, as I'm sure you have discovered. Where should that leave us? Still thankful. Like the apostle Paul, even as we wait for God to answer, we should be quick to give thanks even in the most difficult circumstances. So often, I allow trials to steal my joy away and consume my every thought. I forget all of the good work God will do in my life in the pruning and the refining. Remember Paul's words in 1 Thessalonians? Before he commanded us to be thankful in all things, he reminded us to be joyful in all things. Be joyful all the time, or "rejoice always." The book of James also reminds us to count our trials as joy.

"Count it all joy, my brothers, when you meet trials of various kinds, for you know that the testing of your faith produces steadfastness. And let steadfastness have its full effect, that you may be perfect and complete, lacking in nothing." James 1:2-4

I really have a difficult time getting past that "pure joy" part! When I think of "pure joy" a lot of things come to mind. Puppies, chocolate covered espresso beans, a white beach under a blue cabana, a large pepperoni pizza...the list could go on and on. Never in my human, sinful mind would I ever connect trials and hardship with "pure joy." But that is James's, and Paul's, admonition to us.

Why? Why should we consider it pure joy to suffer? Because we can *know* that God is doing His good work in us, that He is refining, growing, and maturing us. James reminds us that when we go through those life-altering trials or simply the day-to-day challenges, God will develop steadfastness or perseverance in our lives, leading to maturity. When the words "perfect and complete" are used in this verse, James is not indicating that we will be sinless and perfect in the way we tend to think. He is simply telling us that God will use the difficult seasons in our lives to bring us to maturity. We are to endure in thankfulness, considering it all joy.

Joy is a funny thing. No pun intended. Joy isn't happiness...happiness is fleeting. A new pair of shoes or sparkly earrings or a handcrafted espresso can make me pretty happy...for a minute. Things, people, and circumstances can bring us fleeting happiness. But when things break, people fail us, and circumstances change, as they always will, our happiness vanishes with the wind. However, if we find our contentment in the Lord, He will fill us with His lasting joy even in the darkest times.

A key to finding joy in our trials is knowing that God is good, regardless of our circumstances and being grateful for His continued work in us.

I heard a speaker once state that "God has decreed what will bring Him the most glory in our lives." I thought on that for quite some time. I thought back to the trials we had been through with our son. Months upon months in the hospital, years of ongoing medical needs, life and death struggles that exhausted and grieved us. Yet, looking back, I can see God's hand at work, molding us, changing us, giving us the opportunity to impact others' lives with our story of God's faithfulness. But what if we had chosen bitterness instead of joy? Anger instead of thankfulness? I'm not beginning to say we did it all perfectly, not even close. We are still growing and maturing and have far to go. But truly we did find that the "joy of the Lord is your strength" (Neh. 8:10). He graciously gave us everything we needed.

We get to choose how we respond to trials. We've all been around people that suck the joy right out of a room. Always complaining, never content, nothing is ever good enough, or ever right. I have spent time with people who say they love Jesus and yet are the sourest, crankiest, hardest to please people you've ever been around. Seriously? How does that happen? What a sad, terrible testimony. I'm not talking about the times when we are grieving or gaining our footing through a tragedy. I'm talking about finding joy and contentment in our daily lives. Honestly, there are times when we need to have an attitude adjustment and stop griping! We need to remember what Christ has done for us! We have been rescued!

When we focus on who He is and what He's done, how can we be anything but thankful, joyful people? It should flow out of our lives as fruit of the Spirit's work in us, evidence of our faith.

"But the fruit of the Spirit is...joy..." Gal. 5:22

"And let the peace of Christ rule in your hearts, to which indeed you were called in one body. And be thankful...singing psalms and hymns and spiritual songs, with thankfulness in your hearts to God...giving thanks to God the Father through him." Col. 3:15-17

Paul reminds us in Colossians that we should display joy and thankfulness because we have been rescued and redeemed. The more we remember, the more we know, understand, and love Him, the more we will grow in thankfulness to Him. We must remember and reflect daily on the gospel.

"May you be strengthened with all power, according to his glorious might, for all endurance and patience with joy, giving thanks to the Father, who has qualified you to share in the inheritance of the saints in light. He has delivered us from the domain of darkness and transferred us to the kingdom of his beloved Son, in whom we have redemption, the forgiveness of sins." Col. 1:11-14

These truly are my favorite verses in all of Scripture! We must give thanks because He has qualified us, made us fit, to be partakers of heaven! We have been delivered and literally rescued from danger and brought into His kingdom. We have been transferred from death and darkness to His kingdom of light. Rescued and adopted into His family.

"...in love he predestined us for adoption as sons through Jesus Christ, according to the purpose of his will." Eph. 1:5

We have been rescued, delivered, bought, redeemed, and adopted. Whenever I read these passages, my thoughts always go back to our adoption. Several years ago, our family traveled to Orissa, India, to rescue a little girl named Shasmita, who was found beside a road at only a few months old. She was born into a part of India where Christians are horrifically persecuted and where the poverty is staggering. Children, thousands upon thousands of them, wander the streets, starving, homeless, hopeless. God enabled us to rescue this little girl from a dark, dangerous place where violence was rampant. She was only four years old when she came to us and was so tiny and scared. We took her to our hotel that first night and gave her a bath...her very first bath. She thought we were killing her. Picture if you will trying to get a cat into a tub of water. That's pretty much how it went for Shas's first bath. When we finally conquered bathing, we put cool, yellow princess pajamas on her and tucked her safely into a soft bed. For the first time in her life, she knew what it was like to be clean, have shoes, her own clothes, and all the food she could eat. She quickly learned what it meant to be held, loved, treasured, and wanted. To be safe, to belong, to be adopted, to have a family...and to never again be alone.

That's an inadequate word picture for what Christ has done for us! A *million times more* He has rescued us from darkness! He came from His perfect place in heaven to this sinful earth and picked us up out of our dirty, poverty-stricken state. He paid our adoption price with His blood on the cross. The debt of sin we could never pay on our own was canceled and we were redeemed! Our ransom was paid on Calvary's hill and through faith in Jesus we have been set free. When He saves us, He gives us the best bath we could ever have... He washes us white as snow, our sins are gone (Is. 1:18). He puts on us His robes of righteousness and His garments of salvation (Is. 61:10). And we are held, loved, treasured, wanted, and safe. We are adopted into His heavenly family, and we belong...never again alone.

"...having forgiven us all our trespasses, by canceling the record of debt that stood

against us with its legal demands. This he set aside, nailing it to the cross."
Col. 2:13-14

Our debt is canceled; our sins nailed to the cross. How on earth can we not be thankful?

For many months after Shasmita came home, as she struggled to learn her new language and surroundings, she would express her gratefulness to us. She remembered where she had come from and she was profoundly thankful for her family. Every little thing I would do for her, she would look up at me with her sparkly brown eyes and a big smile and say, "Thank you, Mommy, food!" or "Thank you, Mommy, clothes!" or "Thank you, Mommy, bath!"

If I gave her breakfast, tied her shoes, combed her hair, or got her dressed, she gushed her thankfulness. It still moves me to tears to remember. Because all I have to do is look to my adoption into His family and realize I sorely lack that overwhelming gratefulness. Oh, that I would spend less time complaining and more time simply saying, "Thank You, Jesus, rescue!" "Thank You, Jesus, adoption!" "Thank You, Jesus, forgiveness!"

Jesus: the Perfect Thankful Heart

Even as Gethsemane and Calvary loomed before Him, Jesus lovingly partook of Passover with His disciples. He was fully aware that Judas would betray Him, the disciples would desert Him, and Peter would deny Him. He dreaded the pain, the anguish, and the lonely, agonizing death that was now only hours away. The impending trial, the mocking, the beating, the ripping of His beard, and shredding of His flesh. The nails, the crown, the spear. He knew.

And yet He calmly reclined at the table in the Upper Room with His beloved disciples and gave thanks for the bread and wine. The bread that symbolized His crucified body, the wine that symbolized His shed blood.

"And he took a cup, and when he had given thanks he said, "Take this, and divide it among yourselves. For I tell you that from now on I will not drink of the fruit of the vine until the kingdom of God comes." And he took bread, and when he had given thanks, he broke it and gave it to them saying, "This is my body, which is given for you. Do this in remembrance of me." Luke 22:17-19

And the Lamb of God, who would soon take upon Himself the sins of the world, thanked His Father, who would turn His face from His Son, for the bread and the wine that symbolized His death.

"...who for the joy that was set before him endured the cross, despising the shame, and is seated at the right hand of the throne of God." Heb. 12:2

He endured with joy, thanking His Father for the symbols of His broken body because He knew it was the only way of salvation. It was the only way to reconcile sinful man with a holy God. The Savior of the world looked with joy at His suffering because it meant our redemption, our rescue, and our freedom.

Thank You, Jesus, cross.

CHAPTER FIVE

A Trusting Heart

"Blessed is the man who remains steadfast under trial,
for when he has stood the test he will receive the crown of life,
which God has promised to those who love him." James 1:12

"When concern comes to not believing God's promises, it becomes sin."
Jack Hughes

I have most certainly found in my journey of faith that when I choose to walk with a thankful heart through the dark valleys, it is much easier to lean into Him and trust His plan for me. There is great peace to be found resting in Him, knowing He is in control, and understanding I don't have to know the outcome of my trial. God desires for us to have a peaceful, trusting heart even when our circumstances are scary, unpredictable, and seem to be spinning out of control. His Word tells us:

"God gave us a spirit not of fear but of power and love and self-control." 2 Tim. 1:7

He doesn't want us to be consumed with worry, but rather longs for us to trust Him. Maybe you feel like I do—that God seems to give you plenty of special opportunities to see if your faith is genuine and if you truly trust Him. One of those special times for us took place several summers ago. We had been working on the adoption of our daughter for nearly a year and were frustrated and discouraged. I realize now that what we were going through is par for the course on an adoption journey. A lot of hurry up and wait. Adoption is not for cowards or the impatient!

We had expected to travel to India in the spring of 2008, but our papers were held up by our Indian judge who broke his arm and couldn't seem to find the strength or motivation to sign our papers with his other hand. It was ironic to me that our thirteen-year-old daughter, McKenzie, had broken her arm about the same time, yet she managed to finish the school year, handwriting and all. But we found out quickly that this was pretty typical behavior from foreign government officials. We were especially frustrated because we had taken several months off of touring to be able to stay close to home the first few months Shasmita was with us. So instead of traveling that summer, we did home projects, had lots of family time, and waited for word from India.

The call came in July that our papers had been signed and our court date was set. We were ecstatic to finally plan our travel dates! As we prepared for our trip, more than once Joel and I discussed the fact that the region where Shas lived was not necessarily a warm, fuzzy place for Americans or Christians. We joked that we were going on a covert rescue mission. We had no idea how accurate that would become literally hours after our arrival in India.

The flights to New Delhi were uneventful and we were picked up by our interpreter and in-country liaison, Rajeev. He was delightful and kind and put us at ease immediately. The day after our arrival we boarded a flight with another American couple, Mike and Jill, adopting their daughter, Sova, from the same orphanage. We were flying to the eastern state of Orissa (now called Odisha) several hundred miles away on the Bay of Bengal. As we boarded our flight we began to hear comments about violence breaking out in Orissa....a possible assassination and bombings. My heart filled with dread as we passed over the dark expanse below, wondering what would meet us in Orissa.

We felt the tension as soon as we disembarked. Unlike the airport in Delhi, filled with smiling, friendly, noisy travelers, this small airport held suspicious, unfriendly glances and soldiers with AK-47s. We quickly found our drivers and headed to the hotel. Rajeev informed us that there had indeed been an assassination of a radical Hindu leader. The Christians in the region had been blamed and Hindu extremists had taken to the streets in violence.

We were supposed to leave for the half hour long drive to the orphanage in the morning to get Shas and Sova, but it was looking doubtful. A strike had erupted and cars were not allowed on the streets. Furthermore, we were told, being Americans, that if we left the hotel there was a good chance that we would be harmed. As morning dawned after a fitful night's sleep, we turned on the television to horrifying scenes of riots and complete chaos. Churches were burning; cars and tires were on fire in the streets. And it was quickly escalating. We watched reports of an orphanage burning with children inside. We had no reference for where these things were happening and prayed it wasn't our orphanage and that our precious girls were safe. We found out months later, through the Voice of the Martyrs, that over 100 Christians were killed during that time and more than 50,000 were displaced, forced from their homes.

I remember praying as we waited in agony, "Lord, why now? Why couldn't we have traveled when we were supposed to several months ago? We would be safe at home with our family now!" It didn't make sense to me. I was afraid, trying not to panic as the news got worse throughout the day. We wondered if we would leave three orphans at home in our quest to rescue one in India. We wrote letters to our family and got on our knees. It was a time of great emotional upheaval for me, and I realized I had a choice to make. I could panic, cry, and try to make a plan for every possible worst-case scenario. *Or* I could trust. Full out, no-holds-barred trust. Completely placing it in my Father's capable, loving hands.

Now you need to understand, I've been a world-class, professional-level worrier much of my Christian life. There have been many times when my sweet husband has gently reminded me that "worry is a sin." So to be in this dangerous, volatile situation and *not* worry was going to take an act of God and some serious self-control on my part. But I have to tell you: God came through and was so incredibly near and faithful. Even as our situation remained unsure and unsafe, we had complete peace that we were right where God intended us to be. In fact, as we hid in our hotel waiting for the riots to settle down, Rajeev invited us to his room to use his computer to let our families know we were safe for the moment. During that time, God created the perfect, private moment for Joel to share the good news of the gospel with Rajeev. We both had the blessing of kneeling next to the bed in that tiny hotel room beside Rajeev and praying with him as he gave his life to Jesus. God's timing and plan is perfect. If we had gone to India at our planned time, we would have missed the opportunity to live out our faith during a crisis as a testimony to Rajeev, and we possibly would not have had those quiet moments with him. For safety reasons, we were unable to talk openly in the coffee shop or the car with Rajeev to share Christ with him. God knew in advance what the big picture entailed, and it was far more than rescuing a tiny four-year-old girl. He cared so much for Rajeev's soul that he prepared a way for him to hear the truth and have the blinders taken from his eyes.

Never has Isaiah 55:8-9 meant more to me than during those uncertain days in India.

"For my thoughts are not your thoughts, neither are your ways my ways, declares the Lord. For as the heavens are higher than the earth, so are my ways higher than your ways and my thoughts than your thoughts."

God had an eternal plan in mind when He sent us to India. It was so much bigger than we could have imagined! We could only see a tiny sliver of the immediate circumstances. We had to trust that He had a purpose and would remain faithful no matter the outcome of our situation. We saw prayer after prayer answered on that adventurous trip. In fact, the day it was deemed "safe enough" to travel to the orphanage to get the girls, we were still feeling the tension and nervous about leaving our hotel. Our friend, Mike, Sova's daddy, prayed specifically that morning that it would rain hard and keep people off of the streets, thus preventing them from looking into our car. We all laughed in astonishment as a monsoon rain swept in right before we left, pounding our hotel. The wind was wailing, and the trees whipped frantically as the rain fell in sheets. The streets were nearly deserted (which is unheard of in India!) as we made the drive to the orphanage. Literally, as we pulled up to the gates, the rain stopped and the sun popped out. It was the only rain we experienced the whole trip. God is *amazing*. He is in control and even the wind and rain are at His disposal, waiting on His command.

I wish I could say since the day we returned home safely, I have completely learned my lesson on worry and God's trustworthiness and it's no longer ever an issue for me. Sadly, it seems to be one of those issues I have to learn time and again. It's a daily battle of the mind and heart to trust and believe that God has been and will remain faithful. The difficulties we face in this life do not mean that God isn't good. Our idea of "good" and God's idea of "good" are often going to be different. He sees the whole picture and He knows the maturity and growth we will have in our lives as we face trials.

I have several dear friends who are going through desperate, overwhelming trials right now. Each situation is different—from children fighting for their lives in the hospital, to chronic or terminal illness, prodigal children, violent spouses, crumbling marriages, financial ruin. Maybe you are going through one of those life-altering crises. I don't know exactly why we go through all of the hard things. I only know that God *does* have a plan and is and *will be* faithful and He *will* give us the strength we need to endure. In a later chapter we will dig into His promises of hope to us in the storms of life. There are times when there seems to be no end in sight, no light at the end of the tunnel, and we simply and only must cling to the truths of Scripture and the character of God. Be encouraged as you read about the compassion, faithfulness, and character of our God!

"The Rock, his work is perfect, for all his ways are justice. A God of faithfulness and without iniquity, just and upright is he." Deut. 32:4

"...God is love." 1 John 4:8

"God is not a man, that he should lie, or a son of man, that he should change his mind." Num. 23:19

"...what is impossible with men is possible with God." Luke 18:27

"For the Lord your God is a merciful God. He will not leave you..." Deut. 4:31

"The Lord, the Lord, a God merciful and gracious, slow to anger, and abounding in steadfast love and faithfulness..." Ex. 34:6

"The steadfast love of the Lord never ceases; his mercies never come to an end; they are new every morning; great is your faithfulness." Lam. 3:22:23

"For you have been my refuge, a strong tower against the enemy." Ps. 61:3

"The eternal God is your dwelling place, and underneath are the everlasting arms." Deut. 33:27

"...the Lord your God is with you wherever you go." Josh. 1:9
"God is our refuge and strength, a very present help in trouble." Ps. 46:1

"...for he has said, "I will never leave you nor forsake you." So we can confidently say, "The Lord is my helper; I will not fear; what can man do to me?" Heb. 13:5-6

The list of verses showing us, promising us His faithfulness goes on and on! This only scratches the surface!

We hear people remind us "love is a choice" or we have to "choose joy." Both of those statements are true. And so is this one: We choose to trust. We must, by an act of our will, choose to place our hope and trust in our trustworthy God and His faithful, unchanging Word. When we are drowning in uncertainty and mired down in the pit of despair, we need to take our thoughts and worries captive and turn to the book of Philippians. We choose what we will dwell on and these verses have rescued my errant thoughts many times.

"Finally, brothers, whatever is true, whatever is honorable, whatever is just, whatever is pure, whatever is lovely, whatever is commendable, if there is any excellence, if there is anything worthy of praise, think about these things." Phil. 4:8

So, your thoughts that are running rampant like a herd of wild stallions, are they true? Are they pure, honorable, lovely, excellent? If they are true thoughts then they will be based on the truth of God's Word. And the truth is, as we read in those beautiful passages, He will never leave or forsake us. He will never forsake *you*. He is merciful, kind, and full of compassion. His mercies are new every single day. He is slow to anger; He is your refuge, your strength, your helper, your dwelling place, your strong tower, and the God of the impossible. His Word says He is all of these things for His children. And He cannot lie. So what His Word says about Him is unchanging truth. We are commanded to "be anxious for nothing." (Phil. 4:6) It's not a recommendation...it's a direct command. Jesus Himself told His disciples, "...do not be anxious about your life..." (Luke 12:22) I love that He doesn't stop there. He tells His disciples not to worry about what they will eat or wear. Because God takes care of even the birds and the flowers, and we are so much more precious and valuable to Him than birds or flowers. He gently tells His beloved disciples, "Stop your worrying."

God gave me an excellent opportunity to put this command into action several years ago. We live in the country, in the rolling hills of Kansas on acres of woods and pasture. It's truly lovely. We enjoy a variety of wildlife, and our kids have grown up exploring forests, hills, and fields. One crisp fall evening when our boys were about fourteen years old, I was in Nashville recording an album with McKenzie, and Joel was home holding down the fort with the other three kids. Brennan decided it was the perfect evening to head out to the forest and cut down a branch to use for a bow and arrow. He is definitely our outdoor guy and loves pretty much anything that involves tromping around alone in the woods.

Unbeknownst to him, he was not alone in the woods that night. From his perch in the tree, Brennan saw a flash of something out of the corner of his eye. It appeared to be the light tawny color of the many deer that roam the property. He smiled, thinking it would be fun to watch a deer from his vantage point in the tree.

Only it wasn't a deer. He craned his neck as the animal came around a bush. What met his eyes was not the gentle gaze of a doe, but the wicked, golden glare of a large mountain lion! The cougar flattened its ears and hissed as it paced under Brennan's tree, its long tail swishing angrily. Brennan knew he was in deep trouble. Stuck in a tree, with no cell phone, no weapon, and far enough from home to not be heard shouting for help, he didn't have a lot of options. And he knew once the sun went down, that cat would most likely come right up the tree.

In their years of hunting together in Colorado, Joel had taught Brennan how to respond if he ever encountered a mountain lion, and amazingly, Brennan kept his wits about him and maintained eye contact with the cat every time it circled his tree. The longer the ordeal went, the more apparent it became that it would take an act of God to rescue him. He was stuck in the tree for over an hour, waiting and praying. As dusk started to descend, he watched for his opportunity, and simply prayed, "God, I know you have the power to stop this cat from killing me, and I ask you to do it." When the cat circled into the woods, Brennan leaped from the tree and started to run to a nearby cabin. As he ran through the woods and under a barbed-wire fence, he glanced back to see that cougar standing stock-still watching him. Brennan knew God had stopped the cougar from attacking him. But his ordeal was not yet over and he spent another hour trapped in the cabin with the cat outside the door before it gave up and he finally made it home. All that time Joel assumed Brennan was having a great time, enjoying his typical hike through the woods.

Now this is where my trust issues come in to play. As soon as Brennan made it home and explained to Joel what had happened, they were out the door with their rifles to hunt that cat down! Right about the time they reached the darkening woods, I called Joel's cell to check in with everyone. Joel answered with these words,

"Honey, I can't talk right now! We have a situation, and we've got our guns out."

Okay, seriously? He was going to hang up and leave the conversation there, letting me envision all sorts of horrible scenarios! He was kind enough to quickly fill me in before he hung up. They were in a dangerous situation and he needed to focus.

As I sat in the studio, hundreds of miles away, I had a mighy battle with my thoughts. I had seen what a mountain lion had done to a deer on our property months before. I began to shake, thinking about what could have happened to Brennan. As fear began to consume my out-of-control thoughts, the Lord gently reminded me of what was *true*! I needed to go back to Philippians 4:8 and run my thoughts by *that* measuring stick, not what *could* have happened. Sometimes our minds get stuck in a cycle of "what ifs", and I was there! Yet what was true was that God had miraculously saved our son from a mountain lion attack. As we got more details later and our neighbor saw the huge cat the next day, we realized what a close call it had been and were so grateful for God's protection.

Years ago, a close friend knew I was struggling with worry through a particular trial and she simply texted this wonderful, convicting quote to me:

"Worry is sin; a black, murderous, God-defying, Christ-rejecting sin; worry about anything, at any time whatever. We will never know victory over worry and anxiety until we begin to treat it as sin. For such it is. It is a deep-seated distrust of the Father, who assures us again and again that even the falling sparrow is in his tender care."
Charles G. Trumbull

Wow. Worry is a deep-seated distrust of the Father. I didn't like thinking of my "little" worry problem that way, but it's true. When I am consumed with anxiousness and worry, I am not trusting God's plan and faithfulness in my life.

Our circumstances are ever changing. He is never changing. We may not understand what He is doing, why His timing seems so hard, or if the trial will ever end. For some, the trials and pain of this life will only end when they step into the arms of Jesus in eternity. For others the trial will be much shorter, and relief will come here in our days on earth. Truly our responsibility, no matter the length or intensity of the trial, is to trust in His unfailing goodness. In all things.

"Trust in the Lord with all your heart, and do not lean on your own understanding. In all your ways acknowledge him, and he will make straight your paths." Proverbs 3:5-6

Oh, how I want to lean on my own understanding! Trusting and letting go of my expectations and desires is so hard! But I have to choose to lean on Him, place my trust in Him.

Not on my circumstances, my family, friends, or anything else that can fail me or disappoint me.

One of our pastors has recently been teaching through 1 Kings and we have been studying the story and life of Elijah. What an amazing prophet and man of God! Elijah was the first in a long line of prophets that God sent to Israel and Judah. God's people were in rebellion, worshipping Baal, and were in a spiritual and moral downward spiral. In 1 Kings 17, Elijah bravely strode right into Baal-worshipping King Ahab's court and declared that there would be no more rain. Elijah told the king that there would be a severe drought, and then he immediately left town. God sent him out into the desert to live by a brook and be supernaturally fed by ravens. When the brook began to dry up, Elijah was sent to live with a widow and her son, where God miraculously provided for them. Even when the barrels of flour and oil were empty, God simply kept refilling them. God even used Elijah to raise the widow's son from the dead when he suddenly died of an illness. Elijah was living a miracle every single day watching God provide!

After three years of supernatural provision, God sent Elijah back to King Ahab. To say that Ahab was not thrilled to see Elijah is a vast understatement. In Ahab's eyes, Elijah is the troublemaker who caused all of the disaster, famine, and drought in his kingdom. Not at all deterred or intimidated, with great strength, boldness, and complete trust in his God, Elijah challenged Ahab to a showdown with the prophets of Baal on Mount Carmel. He dared them to make an altar and to get Baal to answer with fire from heaven. Those hundreds of frenzied prophets of Baal danced, wailed, and shouted to their god for hours with no answer, no voice, and no fire. Elijah mocked them and told them to call louder, for maybe Baal was sleeping! They screamed, leaped about, and cut themselves for hours. Still no answer, no fire.

Finally, Elijah called the people near. He fixed the altar, set up twelve stones signifying the twelve tribes of Israel, and prepared the altar with wood and the bull sacrifice. Right when it seemed as if he was done, he called for gallons upon gallons of water to be poured over the altar, completely drenching his sacrifice. When all was ready, Elijah humbly and quietly came before the Lord, the God of Abraham, Isaac, and Israel, and asked for His answer. He asked that God would show Himself to His people.

Immediately, fire rained down from heaven and engulfed the altar! There was no wailing, cutting, screaming, and dancing that needed to be done for the holy God of heaven to hear His prophet. God sent blazing fire that consumed the wood, sacrifice, water, and even the altar made of stone. All of it, gone! There was no doubt where the fire had come from, and the people fell on their faces before God.

As soon as the fire was over, God commanded Elijah to kill all the prophets of Baal, all 450 of them. When Elijah finished killing the prophets, he told Ahab he had better hurry home because the rain was coming. After three years of no rain, at the word of Elijah, rain would come.

The story of Elijah is incredible! It's an exciting account filled with miracles and God's provision for His beloved prophet. Elijah had seen and experienced firsthand God's power and protection. And yet, when we get to 1 Kings 19, we see a different side of this man of God. Wicked, conniving Queen Jezebel entered the scene, insanely angry that her prophets of Baal were gone. She was incensed and put a bounty on Elijah's head. At this point, Elijah had every single reason to trust God. God had miraculously provided for him, fed him, brought fire from heaven, and opened up the heavens with rain after so many years of drought. And yet, the words of one nasty woman sent our prophet running for his life! He didn't trust, even after all that had happened, that God would protect him.

"Then he was afraid, and he arose and ran for his life..." 1 Kings 19:3
What in the world? Why, after all God had done in prov-

ing Himself faithful, would Elijah be terrified and run away? It's easy to point the finger at Elijah and shake our heads. And yet... How many times have I seen God's amazing provision, even miracles in my life, yet when the going gets tough again, I react in despair and disbelief. Elijah was exhausted, lonely, hungry, and depressed. He literally lay down under a tree to die and asked God to take his life.

I have felt that way, haven't you? Even after great spiritual victories and firsthand accounts of God's faithfulness, I can easily find myself back in the valley of disbelief, ungratefulness, and discontentment. Much like the children of Israel when they wandered in the wilderness for forty years and God provided for and protected them over and over...and then something would seem hard and they would complain and whine and forget. Too often I complain and whine and forget about God's amazing faithfulness. I forget His compassion and forgiveness and steadfast love. Oh, He longs for us to remember His goodness and mercy to us. To recall and dwell on His wonderful works and deeds that He has recorded in His Word and performed in our lives!

There are many psalms that recount God's faithfulness and provision for His people. They are called historical psalms, written to remind of God's past acts on behalf of His people. The psalmists knew we are prone to wander and forget. It is good for us to read these psalms and see what God has done for His people in the past. Listen first to Asaph and then David's words of encouragement:

"Give ear, O my people, to my teaching; incline your ears to the words of my mouth! I will open my mouth in a parable; I will utter dark sayings from of old, things that we have heard and known, that our fathers have told us. We will not hide them from their children, but tell to the coming generation the glorious deeds of the LORD, and his might, and the wonders that he has done...that the next generation might know them, the children yet unborn, and arise and tell them to their children, so that they should set their hope in God and not forget the works of God, but keep his commandments." Ps. 78:1-7

"Oh give thanks to the LORD; call upon his name; make known his deeds among the peoples! Sing to him, sing praises to him; tell of all his wondrous works! Remember the wondrous works that he has done, his miracles, and the judgements he uttered."
Ps. 105:1-2, 5

These psalms go on and on in remembrance of specific acts that God had done for His people. His deliverance, His victories, His steadfast love. We are not only to remember what God has done but we are to be faithful to pass it down to our children and the generations to come behind us. Our kids need to hear stories of God's faithfulness and care for us. They need to see our reliance on a trustworthy God modeled before them so that when they are grown they will remember. It is good to rehearse, to ourselves and to our children, all the ways that God has provided, protected, and rescued us. It not only encourages our hearts to remember God's past faithfulness, it encourages their faith to grow.

I was recently reading a blog by Paul Tripp. These words jumped off the page and into my heart:

"Here's the conclusion I've come to: no matter how theologically trained my brain is, my heart is still prone to forget. So once more today, I will remind myself of the truths of the Bible, not because my brain needs to be taught a new concept, but because my wandering heart needs to be ushered back into the throne room of grace."
Paul David Tripp

That's me. My wandering heart needs to be ushered back to His throne room, remembering Who He is and what He's done.

I think that's why God puts so many amazing stories in His Word of regular people who have persevered through unthinkable trials. One story that has deeply encouraged me is the biblical account of Daniel. What an incredible man of faith! With so many stories of people in Scripture, we see both their strengths and their failures. This isn't the case with

Daniel. There is no record of failure or sin in Daniel's life. Not that he was perfect, but Scripture records Daniel's story as a great man of faith and focus, steadfastly serving his God. Daniel was wise and righteous and resolved to do nothing to defile himself. He was a young man, only around fifteen years old, when his country of Judah was conquered and he was kidnapped and taken to a foreign land. Only the best and brightest young men of the noble families were taken into captivity and carted away, over 900 miles from home.

Daniel and several of his friends determined that they would not defile themselves with the king's food or wine, and they courageously held fast to their faith and convictions. Can you imagine the pressure on these teenagers? Captive in a land hostile to their God, they refused to give in to the ungodly culture. Daniel realized he was not at the mercy of his circumstances and he fully believed God would be faithful to him and his friends.

So often we let our circumstances and our emotions control us instead of our knowledge of Who God is—faithful, unchanging, the Great I AM. I'm sure Daniel must have struggled with his emotions and fear, far from his family and home, in a land of foreign gods and language. Yet we see, early in Daniel's young life, a resolve and deep commitment to his faith, no matter what the cost. Daniel's faith was not a conditional faith. Conditional faith gives our circumstances the power to dictate God's character: If our circumstances are good, God is good. If everything is falling down around me and my life is imploding, God is no long trustworthy and faithful. Daniel did not have a conditional faith. He believed that God's character was unchanged regardless of his own circumstances. He would trust, believe, and obey God, no matter what the outcome.

The story of Daniel doesn't end with his decision not to eat the king's food. He lived out the rest of his life in captivity, spending his entire adult life in a foreign land. And as an old man in his eighties, still serving foreign kings, Daniel's enemies sought to destroy him. Daniel had proved himself so faithful that King Darius planned to set him over the entire kingdom. This enraged the other officials with jealousy and hatred, and they looked for a way to bring him down. Unfortunately for them, Daniel was so faithful and so diligent in his job, they could find nothing against him. The only thing they could think of was to make it illegal for him to pray to his God. Because they knew he would never compromise on worshipping his God.

So those wicked men went to the king, played to his pride, and goaded him into making a decree that prohibited prayer to anyone but the king. Oh, that sounded great to King Darius! Of course everyone should pray to him for thirty days! King Darius even signed into law that anyone praying to any man or god except himself would be thrown immediately into the lions' den. I love Daniel's calm response to all of this. I wonder if he smiled and shook his head at their schemes. He had seen God's faithfulness over and over through the years. His steadfast confidence in his trustworthy God never wavered. He didn't panic, freak out, or decide to sneak around, praying in secret instead of up by his window like he'd always prayed. No, Daniel remained faithful, making the trek up to his window that faced his beloved Jerusalem. Three times a day, that committed old man knelt slowly by the window, his face set toward the holy city and he prayed to his God.

Well, you know the story. Within hours, Daniel found himself in a pit full of rangy, hungry lions. He was prepared to face whatever consequence would come. There was no room for compromise in his life. With a peaceful, trusting heart he entered that den to face what should have been a horrifying, excruciating death, torn to pieces by ravenous beasts. But God had other plans for this great man. He simply shut the lions' mouths. I don't know if He took away their appetites or put the big kitties down for a little nap, but whatever He did, the Creator and supreme God of the universe supernaturally preserved and rescued His prophet. God was faithful, and

Daniel had harbored no doubt that He would be.

Now, Daniel had no guarantee that God would save him. He didn't know ahead of time if he would live or die. But in his unshakeable faith he understood that God would be with him and keep him, whether to life or to death. There's that unconditional faith. The faith that says, "Though he slay me, I will hope in him..." (Job 13:15)

And like Daniel, we get to choose. Whether we are faced with devastating trials or the day-to-day grind of life, we will either remain unwavering in our faith, persevering, and holding fast to the truth; or we will give up and lose hope in our great God.

Jesus: the Perfecter of Our Faith

"...let us run with endurance the race that is set before us, looking to Jesus, the founder and perfecter of our faith, who for the joy that was set before him endured the cross, despising the shame, and is seated at the right hand of the throne of God. Consider him who endured from sinners such hostility against himself so that you may not grow weary or fainthearted." Heb. 12:1-3

While the account of Daniel and other great stories of faith will challenge us and encourage us, the only perfect example of faith is that of our Savior. Jesus, the author, finisher, and perfecter of our faith lived out a perfect life of trust in His Father during His years on earth. Fully God and fully man, Jesus did not use His divine powers for Himself while living among us. He trusted His heavenly Father as He lived out His daily life. The very fact that Jesus prayed is evidence that He lived by faith, trusting His Father.

And as He "endured the cross, despising the shame" He trusted in His Father's will.

"Father, if you are willing, remove this cup from me. Nevertheless, not my will, but yours, be done." Luke 22:42

Jesus was not looking forward to the agony that was to come. He dreaded it! He knew it would be excruciating and horrible. And yet, He trusted His Father's plan for the redemption of mankind, and He submitted to that plan to be our once for all sacrifice. The sufferings that our precious Savior faced remind us that we do not suffer alone and that He has gone before us, suffering perfectly in our place. When we compare our trials to what He endured, they are nothing! And we can find great comfort knowing that He understands our needs and our heartache.

"For we do not have a high priest who is unable to sympathize with our weaknesses, but we have one who was tempted in every way that we are, yet was without sin." Heb. 4:15

Our High Priest, who sits at the right hand of His Father, knows our needs, our grief, and our temptations. He has suffered in every way that we can suffer, and He sympathizes with us. He longs for us to come to Him with our burdens, and He will give us rest for our souls.

"Come to me all who labor and are heavy laden, and I will give you rest. Take my yoke upon you and learn from me, for I am gentle and lowly in heart, and you will find rest for your souls." Matt. 11:28-29

"Blessed is the man who trusts in the Lord, whose trust is in the Lord." Jeremiah 17:7

I found a beautiful old hymn recently, written over a century ago that has spoken to my heart and seems the perfect way to conclude this chapter on trust.

He knows, my friend. He knows your burden, your trial, and your pain. You can trust the One Who loves you.

He Knows
By G.W.Lyon

He knows the bitter, weary way
The endless strivings day by day,
The souls that weep, the souls that pray
He knows
He knows

He knows how hard the fight has been
The clouds that come our lives between,
The wounds the world has never seen
He knows
He knows

He knows when faint and worn we sink,
How deep the pain how near the brink
Of dark despair, we pause and shrink,
He knows
He knows

He knows, O tho't so full of bliss!
For tho on earth our joys we miss,
We still can bear it, feeling this,
He knows
He knows

GINGER MILLERMON

CHAPTER SIX

A Hopeful Heart

"For I know the plans I have for you, declares the Lord, plans for welfare and not for evil, to give you a future and a hope." Jeremiah 29:11

"When we lose heart it is as if we are saying,
'My circumstances are bigger than my Savior
and His Word isn't enough.'" Lisa Hughes

I lost something really important in November of 1996. I was shivering on a street corner waiting for the light to change in downtown Denver. Snow was falling and blowing around me, and my heart felt as cold and frigid as the wind. I was walking the two blocks alone to the hospitality house near Children's Hospital. I was emotionally and physically exhausted...that day in the NICU had been particularly hard. Jarrott was sick again, and his vitals and oxygen saturation levels were not good. His doctors had no encouraging words for me that day, and I knew they were giving up. As I stood waiting for the light to turn green, tears streamed down my face. I felt hope slip away.

"He's never going to survive. He will never grow up and get married. If he somehow lives, his life will be so painful. He will never know how special it is to have a twin. He will never know how much we love him and how hard we fought for him." My dark thoughts raced freely through my mind. And my flicker of hope died. My loss didn't happen overnight. It was a

slow, painful process over months of grieving and uncertainty. Over the following weeks, my hopelessness turned into anger toward God. *He* was allowing Jarrott and our family to suffer. Soon my heart was filled with bitterness and misery as I refused to pray and let God's Word comfort my heart. It remains to this day one of the most painful seasons I have ever endured. Thankfully, by God's grace, that season was short and even before God began to miraculously heal Jarrott, I came to a place of accepting His plan for our family. God allowed me to understand and trust that He would be good, even if our son didn't survive.

Hope. Think about that word for a minute. What a vital, significant word! Where are we without hope? What happens when we lose it? Speaking from experience, when hope is lost, it is a quick decline into misery and despair. An old Italian proverb says, "Hope is the last thing ever lost." We need hope.

I have a friend named Lindsay who is a personal "hope hero" of mine. She exudes hope and humor when most people would curl into a little ball and whimper. She is brave, funny, and honest about her struggles and why she has reason to hope. In her mid-thirties, Lindsay was a normal, busy mom with four adorable young kids…until an evening in November 2012 changed her life forever. She was routinely giving the kids a quick bath when a shadow suddenly went over her left eye. It was significant enough that she went right in for an exam, and surgery was scheduled for what was thought a retinal tear. Upon further examination early the next morning as she was prepared for surgery, she was told that there was no tear. She was sent home with no answers and by that evening her vision was gone in her left eye. Over the next several days, tests were run, and they finally got news.

"It's MS," were the doctor's quiet words to her, over the phone. In those few words, that diagnosis of multiple sclerosis, her world was changed forever. Doctors' appointments, medications, tests, and road trips to countless more doctors' appointments became her new life. All while she juggled being a wife and mom...with one eye. As she started treatments, including massive doses of steroids, she heard over and over from her health providers, "Just be glad you don't have NMO!" NMO, Neuromyelitis Optica or Devic's Disease, she came to find out, is a super rare, relapsing autoimmune disease that is far worse and harder to treat than multiple sclerosis.

Thankful she "only" had MS, Lindsay learned to drive and function with one eye. She has an amazing sense of humor and started to call herself the "One-Eyed Wonder." I marveled again and again at her steadfast faith and ability to be positive in the midst of great uncertainty and pain. The following is a blog entry that she wrote a few months after she lost her eye.

"Listen. People have two choices when facing a trial.

1. Lay down, have a pity party, be depressed and let it eat you up day after day.
2. Or, choose joy. Because just as love is, joy is also a choice.

Now, that's not to say that when you face a trial you won't go through the occasional pity party (been there), suffer a little depression (done that), and just want to completely give up (totally understand), because you will. I just want the overarching theme of my life to be joy & hope—both things I am blessed to know ONLY come through Christ alone. I have to choose joy, daily. The world tells me I should feel sorry for myself. The world doesn't know that I still have one good eye. That all my limbs, though numb, still function properly. That I can still speak. The world doesn't know that no matter what my or your physical circumstances are, there is HOPE! Romans 15:13 "May the God of hope fill you with all joy and peace as you trust in him, so that you may overflow with hope by the power of the Holy Spirit."

What an incredible, unstoppable attitude! Then, on her tenth wedding anniversary, nearly six months after losing her left eye, she lost vision in her right eye as well. In one fell swoop, she was legally blind. Completely blind with four small children, told she would never drive again, never see her children's faces as they grew up.

More tests followed and it was finally discovered that she didn't have MS after all. Instead, she had NMO. The dreaded disease she was so thankful she thought she didn't have. She started all new treatments, went through plasmapheresis and will be on chemotherapy for the rest of her life. The side effects at first were horrific. She was in a hospital far from home and family, yet she kept fighting and never gave up hope. After being told the nerves in both eyes were pale and dead and that her vision loss was permanent, during her treatment she suddenly regained vision in one eye! What a difference one eye makes! She is able to drive again and keep up with her busy household. She has laughingly told me she can even see the boogers the kids leave on the couch now. It's the little things. She wrote later:

"Two doctors told me the nerves in my eyes were pale and dead. God had other plans. Isaiah 63:7 says, "I will tell of the kindness of the Lord, the deeds for which He is to be praised, according to all the Lord has done for us."

Hope. It's always too soon to give up. You never know what God is going to do.

Hope is often viewed as a temporary illusion. We typically think of hope as a desire for some future thing or happening, which we are uncertain of attaining. It's a vague feeling of desire. We aren't certain something will happen but we sure *hope* it does! Such as, I *hope* my coffeepot will start on time every morning before I wake up. When we hope for something we have at least a little confidence that it will happen. We anticipate the possibility that something we desire *could be* true. There's at least a chance anyway.

Well, here's the great news about the true hope that we have! It's not some nebulous, uncertain longing floating around out there. It's a sure thing, a done deal. When we have a biblical hope versus a vague desire or anticipation, it has nothing to do with chance or our feelings. Our hope is an absolute assurance, a strong and confident expectation. Biblical hope has, as its foundation, all of God's Word, God's unchangeable character, and the completed work of Christ for us on the cross. We are promised as children of God that we do, indeed, have hope. We have hope in His promises, hope in His faithfulness, hope in our trials, and hope in our future.

Because of Who Christ is, and what He has done for us at Calvary, we are never without hope. Because of who we are in Christ and the promises that are ours in Him, we are never without hope. Before we knew Christ, it was an entirely different story. The apostle Paul explains in Ephesians 2 that at one time, we were unclean, separate from Christ and excluded from citizenship. "Having no hope and without God in this world." (Eph. 2:12) That is the description of us before Christ. That is our former state: excluded, left out, and completely hopeless. Have you ever been on the outside looking in? Left out and excluded? I have. I'm sure at one time or another, we all have. It's a terrible, lonely feeling. But when we came to know Him, we were brought near to Him, and He is our peace.

"But now in Christ Jesus you who were once far off have been brought near by the blood of Christ. For he himself is our peace..." Eph. 2:13-14a

We were once separated from Christ with no hope. But through His once for all sacrifice, we are reconciled! Only Christ breaks down the walls and unites us as His, giving us a new identity.

I absolutely love the book of Ephesians. It is one of my favorites. When I am feeling down, succumbing to despair, Ephesians is the perfect place to go to remember who I am in Him. There is such hope in our identity in Christ! Here are a few of our reasons to hope because of our identity:

We are blessed with every spiritual blessing in Christ. (Eph. 1:3)

We are holy, blameless, and covered by God's love. (Eph. 1:4)

We are adopted as His precious children. (Eph. 1:5)

He has freely given us His glorious grace. (Eph. 1:6)

Our sins are taken away, and we are forgiven. (Eph. 1:7)

He has LAVISHED the riches of God's grace on us. (Eph. 1:7-8)

He has made known His plan of salvation to us through Christ. (Eph. 1:9)

We have an inheritance through Him. (Eph. 1:11)

We are sealed for salvation by the Holy Spirit as a promise. (Eph. 1:13)

God's immeasurably great power is available to us. (Eph. 1:19)

We have been made alive and saved by His grace. (Eph. 2:5)

We have been raised up to sit with Christ in glory. (Eph. 2:6)

Our salvation is given to us as a gift. (Eph. 2:8)

We are God's beloved work of art, created for good works. (Eph. 2:10)

We have been brought near to God. (Eph. 2:13)

He is our peace and has reconciled us to one another and to our holy God. (Eph. 2:14)

We have access to the Father. (Eph. 2:18)

We are members of God's household, no longer excluded and left out. (Eph. 2:19)

We can approach the holy God of heaven confidently. (Eph. 3:12)

Now I ask you, in light of all of that, how in the world can we not have hope? How can we despair? We have every reason to persevere in our trials. And yet so often we forget, capitulate to that "spiritual amnesia," and forget who we are. If you are struggling today with hopelessness in your life, are you forgetting your true identity? Go back and remember. It is good to remember what He has done and who we are.

It is also good to remember His promises. Did you know there are thousands of promises in God's Word? 2 Peter 3:9 says,

"The Lord is not slow to fulfill his promise..."

He will keep His Word, His promises to us. God cannot be untrue to His character, and His character is faithful. He has promised that His mercies will be new every single day. I don't know about you, but I need new mercy every day!

"But I call this to mind, and therefore I have hope: The steadfast love of the LORD never ceases; his mercies never come to an end; they are new every morning; great is your faithfulness. "The LORD is my portion," says my soul, "therefore I will hope in him."" Lam. 3:21-23

Jeremiah is reminding us in Lamentations that even during our darkest moments and our deepest sorrows, we have hope because God's mercies are new daily. His compassion toward us will not fail. Even in our sin, we are not consumed because of the great love God has for us as His own children. And He promises that He will continue to be faithful in His forgiveness toward us.

"If we confess our sins, he is faithful and just to forgive us our sins and to cleanse us from all unrighteousness." 1 John 1:9

"He who calls you is faithful; he will surely do it." 1 Thess. 5:24

God is faithful to do what He says He will do. His infinite mercy and compassionate love are greater than any sin in our lives. We can be confident not only in His forgiveness of our sins but in His continued work in our lives. As we grow in our sanctification and come to know and love Him more, our lives should reflect the worthy life that He desires of us. We are called to live lives of holiness and purity (Col. 3) but we simply cannot do it on our own. God is faithful to give us all that we need to live the way He has called us to live.

"His divine power has granted to us all things that pertain to life and godliness, through the knowledge of him who called us to his own glory and excellence, by which he has granted to us his precious and very great promises…" 2 Peter 1:2-4a

He has given us all that we need for life and godliness through His Word and the power of the Holy Spirit that is at work in us. We don't have to wonder if God will equip us to succeed in our Christian walk. We don't have to wonder if our trials will overwhelm or overtake us. The apostle Paul stated in 2 Corinthians 4 that he was afflicted, perplexed, and struck down, but he was not crushed, in despair, or forsaken. God promises to give us everything we need through His divine power, as He did for Paul. We do not walk our path alone! He continues to do His work in us, and even during those times when we feel as if we are making no progress, we can be sure that He is still working.

"And I am sure of this, that he who began a good work in you will bring it to completion at the day of Jesus Christ." Phil. 1:6

Aren't you glad He doesn't give up on us? We aren't finished yet… We won't be until we are face to face with Him in glory. So even in those frustrating times of failure, apathy, and hopelessness, we can know He is working. Because He promised to complete what He started.

When you get discouraged and disheartened, don't forget that God won't give up on you. He won't throw you to the side and decide you are way too high maintenance, way too much work. Honestly, I feel like that sometimes. Like I must be too much work for Him! Surely He must be so disappointed and frustrated with me! When you sharply feel your shortcomings, failures, and past creeping up on you, don't let it steal the joy of your salvation. The joy and assurance of knowing that He is still very much at work in your life, He is still drawing you to Himself and desires a close, intimate walk with you. God's work for us began with Jesus' perfect life, death on the cross in our place, and His defeat of sin, death, and hell. He will continue that work throughout all of our earthly days and finish it when we finally, blessedly, see Him in heaven. Don't despair! He promises to complete His good work in you. And remember, He has good plans for your life. Even if His path looks different than you expected.

"For I know the plans I have for you, declares the Lord, plans for welfare and not for evil, to give you a future and a hope." Jeremiah 29:11

"Why are you cast down, O my soul, and why are you in turmoil within me? Hope in God; or I shall again praise him, my salvation and my God." Ps. 43:5

You know who has the perfect story of hope and perseverance in the Old Testament? Abraham. I love his story of faith and hope. It's an imperfect story, he didn't always trust perfectly, but his name ended up in the Hall of Faith in Hebrews 11, and he is commended for his hope. He was a man whose journey and story definitely looked much different than he expected! Talk about being given high expectations from God Himself and then...nothing for years! Only waiting and hoping and more waiting.

Before his name was changed to Abraham, which means "father of many," he was simply Abram. God appeared to him for the first time when he was seventy-five years old. Living in the land where his father had settled, Abram is suddenly told by God to leave everything he knew and travel to a whole new land, not really even knowing where he was going. God told him he would become a great nation that would be incredibly blessed. Now, I don't know everything there is to know about biblical times, but it seems to me that seventy-five is a little old to be traveling hundreds of miles on foot, or donkey, or anything other than first class on an airplane. On top of that, Abram was childless, and God just promised him that he would be a great nation! And Abram believed every single word. He packed up his tent, his wife, his animals, his nephew, and all their stuff and hit the dirt road. God met him along the way and again promised him that his offspring, his very own children and heirs, would inherit the land they were crossing. Abram believed Him and built an altar. So on they went on their journey.

It was an eventful saga laid out for us in Genesis 12-14. Abram's adventure included greed, lying, wife-snatching, dysfunctional family discord, kidnapping, a daring rescue mission, and more. God's Word is certainly not boring! And Abram's life at seventy-five was ridiculously action packed. Finally, in Chapter 15 of Genesis, God appears to Abram again, this time in a vision. He once more promised Abram a great nation, coming from his own body. A nation that would rival even the innumerable stars Abram could see in the heavens above. And without physical evidence of the child God promised, Abram, in faith, believed.

"And he believed the LORD, and he counted it to him as righteousness." Gen. 15:6

What an incredible, convicting example to us! How many times do we know the promises God gives us of provision, protection, salvation, and hope, and yet…we doubt Him? Too often our faith is so small, based only on what we can see. Not Abram. He believed that God would bring about what He promised. Now, he definitely had his moments of weakness. Like the next chapter when his doubting wife, Sarai, talks him into Plan B, hands over her servant as a surrogate mother, and a disaster ensues. That's usually what happens when we try to "help" the Lord with Plan B...a disaster ensues. Yet God did not give up on Abram and appeared to him again. This time changing his name to Abraham and his wife's name to Sarah. He promised, again, that Abraham would be a great nation, but this time He specifically stated that Sarah would be the mother of that great nation. At this point, Abraham is ninety-nine years old and Sarah is ninety.

Okay, it's really not hard to see why Abraham and Sarah would laugh when God told them they would be parents. These people are old! Romans 4 states bluntly that Abraham's body was as good as dead and Sarah's womb was dead. Can you even wrap your mind around being 100 years old and chasing a toddler? I'm not even halfway there yet and I can't imagine! But with all the odds stacked against them, no humanly possible way for Sarah to have a baby with a dead womb, Abraham maintains his hope and believes what God says.

"In hope he believed against hope, that he should become the father of many nations, as he had been told, "So shall your offspring be." He did not weaken in faith when he considered his own body, which was as good as dead (since he was about a hundred years old), or when he considered the barrenness of Sarah's womb. No unbelief made him waver concerning the promise of God, but he grew strong in his faith as he gave glory to God, fully convinced that God was able to do what he had promised. That is why his faith was counted to him as righteousness." Rom. 4:18-22

He hoped against hope. He believed God even when it seemed hopeless. Even after waiting twenty-five long years to see the promised fulfilled. I don't know about you, but if I have to wait longer than twenty-five minutes sometimes I start to doubt. We will discuss patiently waiting on the Lord in our next chapter, but let me say it is not my strongest character quality and may not be yours either.

How easily we give up when we don't get an immediate

answer or when we feel like we are "100 years" into our trials and there is no end in sight. We need to take a lesson from Abraham's life and simply believe God, hoping against hope, that He is able to do what He promises. We must be fully convinced, fully persuaded that God is powerful enough to fulfill his Word. The One Who promises is faithful.

"Let us hold fast the confession of our hope without wavering,
for he who promised is faithful." Heb. 10:23

Earlier in the chapter, I listed the reasons we have to hope because of our identity in Christ. Here are beautiful, encouraging reasons we have to hope in light of His character and His promises to us:

When we come to Him, He gives us rest. (Matt. 11:28-30)

He will be slow to anger, merciful, gracious and loving to us. (Ps. 103:8)

He has removed our sins as far as the East is from the West. (Ps. 103:12)

His angels camp around us and deliver us. (Ps. 34:7)

He will be our refuge when we cry out to Him. (Ps. 34:17; Ps.107:13-16)

When we seek Him, He hears and answers our prayers. (Ps. 34:4, 6, 15)

He is so near to those whose hearts are broken and crushed. (Ps. 34:18)

He will deliver us from destruction and despair and give us a new song. (Ps. 40:2-3)

He will keep us safe, allowing us to sleep in peace. (Ps. 4:8)

He knows and cares about every tear we cry. (Ps. 56:8)

He gives us a new heart, replacing our heart of stone with a heart of flesh.
(Ezekiel 36:26)

He knows all of our physical needs and will provide. (Matt. 6:31-34; Phil. 4:19)

He will not hold back anything good for us when we walk with Him. (Ps. 84:11)

He promises wisdom, direction, and guidance to us. (James 1:5; Ps. 32:8; Prov. 3:5-6)

He will always provide a way out of temptation. (1 Cor. 10:13)

He will comfort us in all of our trials. (2 Cor. 1:2-4)

As we trust Him, He will keep our hearts and minds peaceful. (Is. 26:3; Jn. 14:27)

There will be an end to our suffering and pain and He will wipe every tear away.
(Rev. 21:4)

This list could go on and on. Literally there are thousands upon thousands of promises. God's Word is true, He will be faithful, and we have every reason to hope. Specifically and most importantly we have every reason to hope because of the finished work of Christ on the cross.

Jesus: Our Perfect Reason to Hope

"There is therefore now no condemnation for those who are in Christ Jesus." Romans 8:1

What beautiful, hope-filled words Romans 8 opens with for us! There is no more condemnation, no more guilt for us because of what Jesus did on the cross. Jesus perfectly fulfilled every aspect of the law in our place because we never could. Then He "canceled the written code (the law) and nailed it to the cross." Because of His work, His death, burial, and resurrection, we have hope.

That alone would be enough, but our reasons to hope in Christ don't stop there. As we have seen in His many promises to us, we are not left on our own to endure and sort out this life. He is present, aware, and compassionate to our needs. And we will never, ever be separated from His care, His protection, and His love for us.

"What then shall we say to these things? If God is for us, who can be against us? He who did not spare his own Son but gave him up for us all, how will he not also with him graciously give us all things?" Rom. 8:31-32

God is on our side! Who could ever defeat or stand against us when we have the holy God of heaven guiding, protecting, and fighting for us with every resource in the universe at His command? What could we possibly fear? God loved us so much He didn't even spare His own precious Son the agony of the cross, because it was the only way we could have redemption, peace, and fellowship with Him. If He loved us that much, surely He will give us all the strength and provision we need!

"Who shall separate us from the love of Christ? Shall tribulation, or distress, or persecution, or famine, or nakedness, or danger, or sword? No, in all these things we are more than conquerors through him who loved us. For I am sure that neither death nor life, nor angels nor rulers, nor things present nor things to come, nor powers, nor height nor depth, nor anything else in all creation, will be able to separate us from the love of God in Christ Jesus our Lord."
Rom. 8:35, 37-39

There is nothing and no one in this world or the spiritual realm beyond that can separate us from His great love. Nothing. No circumstance, no tragedy, no person, and no force of nature. We are sealed, chosen, and adopted. Forever His. You are His precious, beloved, priceless treasure. He cares intimately about every burden you bow under and every tear you cry. He is not immune to your pain, or turning a deaf ear to your cries. Your Heavenly Daddy sees and knows your every heartache. He thinks of you in the tenderest of terms, and much as we long for our children to come to us with their needs and sorrows, He longs for you to come to Him. Broken, defeated, hurting, desperate…whatever it is you are facing and feeling, His arms are open, and He is waiting. Child of God, you are loved! His promises are for you. Come to Him! Don't give up. You have all you need and the truest Source of hope. Jesus reassures us best in His own words:

"…In the world you will have tribulation. But take heart; I have overcome the world."
John 16:33b

Take heart. Don't lose hope. He has overcome.

GINGER MILLERMON

CHAPTER SEVEN

A Patient Heart

"The Lord is good to those who wait for him,
to the soul who seeks him.
It is good that one should wait quietly
for the salvation of the Lord." Lamentations 3:25-26

"The Lord is not slow to fulfill his promise..." 2 Peter 3:9

""Later" is more than "not now."
"Later" means "Listen while you wait.""
Paul Maxwell desiringgod.org

I'm going to be painfully transparent for a minute here. I hate waiting. I am terrible at waiting. I am not a naturally patient person. I hate waiting in line, waiting for a parking space, waiting in the car line at the kids' school, waiting on my ultra slow coffee maker to finally finish brewing (I REALLY hate that), waiting on an anticipated phone call...you get the point.

Life is full of waiting. Waiting on others, waiting on circumstances...waiting on God. I kind of thought by this point in my life I would be a lot better at waiting. That after knowing Jesus for forty years I would be smiling serenely all the time, long-suffering, full of grace and patience. Well, this is not a news flash for my family, but I'm still a work in progress when it comes to patience. I am getting there, making progress...slower than I should. My husband, on the other hand, might be the most patient person on the globe. He has put up with my sinful impatience for years with great compassion, humor, and tolerance.

It still tickles me to remember our first few months after we brought Shas home from India. She knew very little English. In fact, her vocabulary consisted of only three important words: Mommy, Daddy, and cookie. And when you're four, what else do you really need to know? She quickly added the words chocolate and candy to her limited vocabulary. She had quite the sweet tooth. She was the cutest, funniest little delight as she learned English and started to put together phrases and words. There were a lot of giggles at our house.

One evening we were in the car and she started asking for chocolate from the back seat. This was not an uncommon conversation. It was not an appropriate time for a sweet and Joel simply said,

"No, Shas, not right now. It's not time for chocolate now. Maybe you can have chocolate later."

She nodded and lisped, "Chocolate laler." Five minutes passed and she asked, "Chocolate now?"

Joel smiled and replied, "No, Shas. No chocolate yet. You need to be patient."

She got a confused look on her tiny face, scrunched her nose up in disgust and said in her adorably thick accent, "I do not know patient."

What she meant was, "I don't know what the word patient means."

But I laughed and looked at her and said, "Yeah, Shas, I do not know patient either."

Patience is hard. Waiting is hard. And yet living a life of faith, in obedience, is rarely easy, is it? We are commanded to wait, to be patient. Both with people and in our difficult circumstances. And honestly, sometimes they are combined because some people *are* our most difficult circumstance!

"Wait for the LORD; be strong, and let your heart take courage; wait for the LORD!"
Ps. 27:14

"...be patient with everyone." 1 Thess. 5:14 (NIV)

Let's take a moment to explore being patient with people before we spend the bulk of our chapter on waiting and being patient in our circumstances and trials. Obviously, "be patient with everyone" doesn't leave a lot of room to be impatient with people, does it? It's a command. It is required that when we live a life motivated not by guilt or good works, but by our deep love for Christ and what He has done for us, we will, indeed, be patient people. Some of us are not naturally patient. Do we get a pass on that then? Do we receive a "get out of jail free card" because we have Type A "get 'er done" personalities, and it's harder for us? Um, no. I wish. It means we need more grace from our precious Jesus and more time in His Word and prayer, listening to Him, and begging Him for strength and lasting change.

I didn't really know I had a temper until I got married. I know, that sounds terrible, doesn't it? It wasn't Joel's fault. I honestly didn't realize how selfish, self-righteous, proud, and...you get the picture. I'm very thankful I'm not the same person I used to be. After twenty-five years of marriage, God has refined me, knocked off some rough edges, and He continues to buff away on me. If you hang around me much, you'll figure out quickly that I like to laugh, and I am pretty easy to get along with most of the time. You would probably not suspect that as a young pastor's wife, I had an incredibly short fuse in our home. We were a few years into our marriage when God graciously opened my eyes to my grievous sin of anger, impatience, and irritability. I don't remember the exact situation, but one day my sweet, gracious husband gently said to me, "Honey, I never know what's going to set you off. The smallest things just tick you off."

His honest words crushed me. Yet I knew he was right. Something had to change. I was making so much conflict in our marriage. He never knew what to expect from me. It's a wonder he wanted to come home at night! God mercifully ripped off the blinders and let me see my anger and sin. I didn't want to be a contentious wife! A continual drip making him want to run for the rooftop or a desert!

"A continual dripping on a rainy day and a quarrelsome wife are alike…" Prov. 27:15a

"It is better to live in the corner of the housetop than in a house shared with a quarrelsome wife." Prov. 25:24

"It is better to live in a desert land than with a quarrelsome and fretful woman." Prov. 21:19

"Like a gold ring in a pig's snout is a beautiful woman without discretion." Prov. 11:22

"The wisest of women builds her house, but folly with her own hands tears it down." Prov. 14:1

God's Words…not mine! I was lacking discretion and self-control, and my foolishness was tearing up my house. As wives, we would be wise to listen and apply the truths of the Proverbs. We get to choose how we are going to respond when someone speaks hard, constructive criticism to us. We choose whether we will lash out in denial and anger, or we have the opportunity to take their words into consideration and look to see the truth in them. Even if we feel the words aren't justified or aren't completely true, we do well to consider and be humble and teachable. I'm eternally thankful that God patiently and graciously opened my eyes and began to change my heart.

Someone suggested I take the book of Proverbs and slowly meditate and read through every chapter, highlighting and noting each verse that referenced being quick to anger, quick to speak, and quarrelsome. Ouch! It was a painful, pruning process for me! I quickly noted that God looks at a person who is quick to anger as a fool. (Prov. 29:11; 14:29; 14:17; 12:16) I heartily recommend, if you struggle with anger, impatience, and a short fuse, take some time to carefully go through Proverbs. Your heart surely will be pricked as mine was. And that's a good thing. We must have a tender conscience, quick to hear and heed the Holy Spirit's conviction.

And that short fuse and tendency to be quick to anger doesn't only apply to people. It also applies to our circumstances. I know by nature that none of us like to be interrupted or want delays or changes in our plans. We don't like our "to-do lists" to get scrambled or scrapped altogether. We all have a very strong desire for a trouble-free life, and we tend to get irritated and grumpy when our plans go by the wayside. We don't like traffic jams on the highway when we're running late for an appointment or a coffee date with a friend. We don't like car repairs, flat tires, and broken appliances. We don't like for babies to scream or throw up—or both—all night long. We don't like checks to bounce or bank accounts to go dry. We want smooth, predictable days. Days full of freshly ground coffee, soft jazz, and lazy days at the beach. Bottom line, we want things to go our way, according to our plans. And when they don't, and they rarely do, our natural response is to be provoked.

Preaching on 1 Corinthians 13, John Piper said these impactful words in a sermon about love being patient:

"Now Paul says, "Love suffers long...and is not (easily) provoked." So what becomes of this whole side of us that suffers short—has a short fuse—and that is easily provoked and easily complains and easily grumbles and easily gets angry and easily criticizes? The answer is: it must die. To love like this is to die. If I am to be like this, something in me must die. My strong craving for a trouble-free life must die. My need for an uninterrupted schedule must die. My demandingness that frustrations and interference get out of my way must die. We simply cannot love the way Paul describes until we die."" John Piper (desiringgod.org)

Paul also reminds us bluntly that we are to die to sin.

"What shall we say then? Are we to continue in sin that grace may abound? By no means! How can we who died to sin still live in it?" Rom. 6:1-2

If anger and impatience is sin (please study Col. 3 if you're not sure) then it needs to be put to death in our life. Gentleness, long-suffering, and peace should be virtues that define our daily living, even in the most difficult of circumstances. And that means waiting patiently, often on God. Waiting for His perfect plan to unfold. Waiting for His timing in a situation. Waiting for His rescue and intervention. And again, realizing His ways are not my ways, and the answer I so patiently (or impatiently) am waiting for, might not be the answer I had in mind.

The past six months have been the perfect opportunity for me to live this out firsthand. It was only a few days after I finished the rough draft of this book that life as I knew it came to a screeching halt. It was mid-February and our ministry calendar had filled up for the spring with concerts and women's events. I was looking forward to traveling to Florida the following week for a women's conference and had even scheduled in a few minutes at the beach—my favorite, happy place. I was rushing to meet all the deadlines, get everything lined out for the kids while I was gone, and check off my to-do list before life got a little crazy with travel. That crisp winter morning I had just dropped the kids off at school and was driving to meet Joel at the gas station to fill up. I started to feel kind of weak and lightheaded, and as I stopped my car behind his, I slumped over in the seat. Joel looked up to see that something was very wrong. He pushed me into the passenger seat, and drove me the few blocks to the ER. I was in and out of consciousness as my blood pressure dropped, and the hospital staff ran tests and blood work to find the cause. After several hours and inconclusive tests, I eventually stabilized and went home later that day completely exhausted, weak, and with symptoms similar to a mini-stroke.

The next weeks passed in a blur of more tests and doctors appointments, and reality began to set in that I was not going to be able to keep my travel and speaking schedule. Most days I was barely able to get off the couch, my speech sometimes slurred, and my mind often slow and confused. It was with much disappointment that we canceled all of my upcoming events.

I had been diagnosed several months prior with a rare vascular syndrome, but other than chronic pain and fatigue, I was managing to keep up with life. I didn't realize my condition could be something of a ticking time bomb of symptoms, and when things went bad, they quickly went bad!

As the months have passed, some symptoms have eased and others have lingered and slowly gotten worse. I am not able to drive much anymore and am mostly at home, never knowing from day to day how I will feel. This is quite a frustrating challenge for a social person like myself, used to going in 100 different directions usually 100 miles per hour. I have been to many doctors, extensively researched medical journals and forums, documented about my condition, and consulted at the Mayo Clinic. My syndrome has no easy fix, much of it experimental, and often ineffective. As I write these words today, I am still waiting on a call to schedule the surgery I hope might bring a cure and allow me to get back to the things I love and the ministry I feel called to. Did I mention yet that I hate waiting?

So what are we to do when there is no light at the end of the long tunnel of burdensome circumstance, no relief in sight to our trial? We wait on the Lord. We wait patiently for Him. We pray earnestly and we trust. It's much easier said than done, I realize. I have bent low under the agony of waiting and have cried out in sheer frustration and grief, "How long? When will you answer? How much longer?" I have felt the deafening silence when I think my prayers are being overlooked and unanswered. When He is asking me to wait, be patient, and quietly trust Him. When He is giving me the opportunity to grow in grace as I suffer long.

You have probably been there too. The psalmist certainly had. Listen to David's anguish as he cries out to the Lord.

"Save me, O God! For the waters have come up to my neck. I sink in deep mire, where there is no foothold; I have come into deep waters, and the flood sweeps over me. I am weary with my crying out; my throat is parched.
My eyes grow dim with waiting for my God." Ps. 69:1-3

Oh, I feel his pain. I have felt like I was drowning in affliction, my hope dimming as I waited.

"How long, O LORD? Will you forget me forever? How long will you hide your face from me? How long must I take counsel in my soul and have sorrow in my heart all the day? How long shall my enemy by exalted over me?" Ps. 13:1-2

Yet even in his grief, even as he questions, it's as if he takes a deep breath and remembers.

"But I have trusted in your steadfast love; my heart shall rejoice in your salvation. I will sing to the LORD, because he has dealt bountifully with me." Ps. 13:5-6

"Be strong, and let your heart take courage, all you who wait for the LORD!" Ps. 31:24

There will simply be times in our lives that we do not understand what God is doing and why He is taking so long to answer. Times when we have to accept that His answer is "wait" and may even end up being a delayed "no." The bottom line is this: do we trust Him? We have to go back to dwelling on the Philippians 4:8 way of thinking: what do we know is true? We know His Word is true, we know He is faithful and that He has a good plan for our lives. On His timetable, not ours.

"He has made everything beautiful in its time..." Ecc. 3:11

"Oh the depth of the riches and wisdom and knowledge of God! How unsearchable are his judgments and how inscrutable his ways!" Rom. 11:33

"This God—His way is perfect; the word of the LORD proves true;

he is a shield for all those who take refuge in him." 2 Sam. 22:31

"He is the Rock, his works are perfect, and all his ways are just.
A faithful God who does no wrong, upright and just is he." Deut. 32:4

How unsearchable His judgement and inscrutable His ways! When we feel as if He doesn't care or isn't listening or doesn't answer, we need to remember these words. His ways are unfathomable to us. He sees the whole thing, the big picture, and the end result. And its *good*, again, to repeatedly go back and remember how He has provided in our lives during times of uncertainty. For me, all I need to do is remember my frustration and doubt when we were waiting to go to India on *my* timetable. I had it all planned perfectly! And yet God was preparing the heart of a precious Hindu man thousands of miles around the world so that in His time, that man's heart would be ready to receive the good news of the gospel. I wouldn't have missed that moment for anything! God's plan had a bigger, more eternal purpose than I could've imagined! As difficult as it is, we need to wait patiently.

"I waited patiently for the LORD; he inclined to me and heard my cry. He drew me up from the pit of destruction, out of the miry bog, and set my feet upon a rock, making my steps secure. He put a new song in my mouth, a song of praise to our God. Many will see and fear, and put their trust in the LORD." Ps. 40:1-3

These three short verses are a gold mine of hope to me in the waiting! God *will* hear and incline His ear to us. He *will* draw us up from our pit of despair and destruction, the quicksand of defeat that mires us down. He *will* make our steps secure and give us a new song of praise to Him. And best of all? When we wait faithfully, patiently, trusting His plan and His time, others will see our faith and hope in our Savior and they will know they can trust Him as well. Be encouraged! Wait on the Lord! What a privilege to suffer and wait so that we can turn to Him for comfort and be a testimony of His perfect faithfulness.

Before we look to Jesus, our perfect example of a patient heart, let's be encouraged by an Old Testament man who faithfully waited and persevered through unbelievable circumstances.

There are many biblical characters we could study to see a life of patience and perseverance, but this one truly takes the cake.

We have to consider the story of Job. You knew that one was coming, right? You can't talk about patience without pulling out Job's story. Even people who have never picked up a Bible have probably heard or used the phrase; "He has the patience of Job!" And indeed, his is an incredible story of faithful waiting.

Job was a very wealthy man living in the land of Uz thousands of years ago. He had prestige, unparalleled possessions, and a large, loving family. He had thousands of donkeys, oxen, camels, sheep, and servants. He was not only wealthy and respected; he was an upright, godly man. His wisdom and counsel were greatly respected in the land. He was a defender of the poor, the fatherless, the widow, the lame, the defenseless, and the needy. He used his wealth for great good and was a kind, compassionate man. Basically, you would be hard-pressed to ever find a more generous, righteous man. In fact, after Satan had been roaming around the earth, looking to stir up trouble, he came to give an account before God, and the Lord asked him if he had noticed Job.

"Have you considered my servant Job, that there is none like him on the earth, a blameless and upright man, who fears God and turns away from evil?" Job 1:8

Wait; hold up a second here. Can you even imagine in the furthest reaches of your most wild moment of imagination that God would look at your life and say that about you? I can't! I know my myself and my weaknesses all too well! What a faithful man Job must have been that the holy God of the universe would commend him so! God noticed Job's faithful generosity and his desire to please Him. It warmed God's heart to see Job living his life out in compassion and wisdom. This account of God and Satan's interaction in heaven motivates me greatly to strive to live a blameless, upright life! That God would look down from His throne and be pleased with my offering of obedience and righteous living. What a challenge to us!

Ok, back to the story. So, God asks Satan if he has noticed Job's blameless life and here is Satan's quick and disdainful response:

"Does not Job fear God for no reason? Have you not put a hedge around him and his house and all that he has, on every side? You have blessed the work of his hands, and his possessions have increased in the land. But stretch out your hand and touch all that he has, and he will curse you to your face." Job 1:10-11

Satan has absolutely no regard or respect for Job's righteous living and is convinced Job only lives a godly life because God has blessed him so tremendously. He hates everything about Job's generous life and would like nothing better than to destroy it and watch Job suffer and curse God. There are so many aspects to study about this fascinating conversation. God gives us a peek into the spiritual realm here, doesn't He? He lets us understand that Satan is allowed to come before Him and accuse the saints—God's children who are striving to live for Him. It gives us a glimpse of the sheer hatred Satan has for us and shows us his desire to destroy our lives. The Bible tells us that Satan accuses us day and night before God. (Rev. 12:10) He is our adversary, a prowling lion looking for someone to devour. (1 Pet. 5:8) There is no doubt: we have an enemy, make no mistake. So what does God say to Satan's accusations about Job?

"Behold, all that he has is in your hand.
Only against him do not stretch out your hand." Job 1:12a

So there it is. The conversation in heaven that marked the beginning of the disasters that would befall Job's life. Satan left God's presence and began planning his scheme to make Job curse God. Chapter one of this book continues with Satan making his move against Job. All in one day, Job lost all of his livestock, nearly all of his servants, and all ten of his beloved children. The very children he faithfully made sacrifices for, praying for the forgiveness of their sins in case they unwittingly sinned against God. Gone. Everything gone except his wife and his life. All in one, horrible, catastrophic day. Mere words could never describe the loss and anguish heaped upon this godly man. I try to imagine losing one of my children and I can't fathom it. Job's loss takes my breath away.

What will Job's reaction be to these devastating circumstances? What will he say about his God now? Will he curse God to His face like Satan predicted? Look at Job's amazing response:

"Then Job arose and tore his robe and shaved his head and fell on the ground and worshipped. And he said, "Naked I came from my mother's womb, and naked shall I return. The LORD gave, and the LORD has taken away; blessed be the name of the LORD." In all this Job did not sin or charge God with wrong." Job 1:20-22

Unbelievable. Oh, that my heart would respond with a fraction of that trust and faithfulness. Job's situation does not get better, not for a long, long while. After losing all of his possessions and family, Satan is not satisfied and seeks God's permission to attack his health. Job is soon covered in boils, suffering unthinkable physical pain. He wishes he had never been born. I don't blame him.

To add to his suffering, his super supportive wife encourages him to just "curse God and die." (Job 2:9) Sweet, huh? He refuses, and continues to not sin with the words he spoke about his suffering and circumstances. Soon, his friends hear about the events in his life and come to "help." Well, the only helpful thing they did was keep their traps shut for seven days. When they finally began to spew their advice, it was to try to convince Job he deserved his suffering and he must have some horrific sin hidden in his life. They were speaking under the false assumption that suffering is *always* the result of sin. They couldn't fathom that a truly godly man would suffer so. He must've done *something* to deserve all of this! As I mentioned way back in Chapter One, there are times when sin does result in difficult consequences and suffering but it is by no means the only cause. We can learn a great deal from Job's friend's response to him and their lack of comfort.

Job did not suffer and wait perfectly. He reached a breaking point and began to question at length what God was allowing to happen in his life. Job's biggest trial was not losing all of his possessions and family; it was the lack of understanding the *why* in his suffering. He wanted to know why! Do you know what? He never discovered why. We, as readers thousands of years later, are given the premise of his suffering in Job 1. We understand what was happening in the heavens before Job's life fell apart but Job never knew. Toward the end of the book of Job, God spoke to Job out of a mighty storm, plying him with questions of His own. Asking Job questions about the intricacies of creation, showering him with details of the forces of nature at His fingertips. Verse after verse God expounds to Job the unfathomable mysteries of nature, the animal kingdom, and the universe. God's wasn't expecting answers from Job; He was showing Job his ignorance of creation and the moral order of things. His point was this: If Job couldn't understand God's physical creation, how could he think to understand the mind and character of God? He could not. God is sovereign over all. He is sovereign over His creation and He is sovereign over our lives. Job clapped his hand over his mouth and repented of his pride in dust and ashes. (Job 40:4-5; 42:1-6)

Job unquestionably suffered more than we ever will or could ever imagine. If Job, this godly, righteous man, repented of questioning God's sovereignty and justice, how must we respond in our trials? I truly believe we do not have the right to question our almighty God. Is this easy? No. Have I questioned? Yes. And I must learn from Job's mistakes and repent.

I have a dear friend who is, to me, a modern day Job. Maybe you know someone like that. My friend's circumstances are incredible. Even her doctors put her in the rare one-percent on her various medical anomalies. And it's not only her; major medical needs and crises afflict her children as well, which is even worse for a mommy. My friend astounds me. She is the bravest, toughest person I know. She will have a raging fever and infection, be recovering from treatments or whatever the case may be, and she will still be faithful to serve, faithful to minister to her family, faithful to be at her kids' ballgames and events. I would be curled up in a tiny little ball in a dark room. But not my friend! She simply never quits. She is a beautiful example of endurance to me.

She is not waiting and suffering perfectly, and I am not waiting perfectly for her. I find myself praying, "How long, how much, O Lord?" when a new need arises. But she faithfully perseveres. And when her foot stumbles, as all of ours would, she lets the Lord pull her back up out of the mire and draw her close. My friend may never know in this lifetime and on this earth why she has suffered. But she does know that God is just and sovereign, and she can trust in Him. She has felt His comfort; she has seen His people rally to support her. I don't know all of the reasons for her circumstances, but I do know she has challenged me and her faith has strengthened mine.

Maybe you are in much the same place today. Maybe you are suffering and seeking an answer to your "why" question. Friend, instead of asking "why," would you simply rest in Him today? Would you release your need to know and lean on the sovereignty of the God who made you and loves you? Could you accept that you might never get all of your questions answered on this earth? You may never see all of your prayers answered in the way you hope, but that doesn't mean He isn't listening and answering in His time. We have no idea all that is going on behind the scenes! And what a comfort to know that as we wait imperfectly for God to move, His precious Son, Jesus, waited perfectly for us. His perfect righteousness covers our failures as we continue to run our race with perseverance, fixing our eyes on Him. We set aside all that hinders and everything that entangles us, and we run this long distance race faithfully to the finish.

Jesus: The Perfect Example of Patience

"...who for the joy that was set before him, endured the cross..." Heb. 12:2

We don't have to read far into the Gospels before Jesus' gentle patience becomes evident. If you think about it, we see his patience with people even at the early age of twelve. He showed patience and respect to his earthly parents, who knew He was the Messiah, when they were frantically looking for him after Passover. They were shocked to find Him answering questions and astonishing the teachers in the temple. When they expressed their anxiety to Him, young Jesus gently asked,

"Why were you looking for me?
Did you not know that I must be in my Father's house?" Luke 2:49

And then without arguing or getting frustrated with their lack of understanding, Jesus submitted patiently to them and went home. It would be about eighteen long years of waiting and growing before Jesus would start his ministry, not until he was around thirty years old. Years of waiting, doing carpentry work (Mark 6:3) as a simple carpenter's son. (Matt. 13:55.) He was the Creator of the world, God incarnate! And He patiently waited...living and working and serving in a humble existence.

His patience is also displayed many, many times to His disciples. In spite of following Him and sitting at His feet daily for months upon months, they were often slow to learn, thickheaded, and self-centered. They saw Him firsthand heal the lame, give eyes to the blind, cure incurable diseases, feed thousands, and even raise the dead...and they still doubted! I don't know about you, but at some point I would have become pretty frustrated and impatient with them! Jesus occasionally asked rhetorical questions or remarked that they were slow to believe, but He kindly kept guiding and teaching them. All the way to the Garden of Gethsemane, only hours before His crucifixion, He continued to instruct and lovingly teach his beloved disciples. What perfect patience!

And then to the cross, He patiently suffered. Knowing the agony that lay before Him, He willingly endured for us.

"...who for the joy set before him, endured the cross, despising the shame, and is seated at the right hand of the throne of God. Consider him who endured from sinners such hostility against himself, so that you may not grow weary or fainthearted."
Heb. 12:2-3

Through vicious beatings, scorn, shame, temporary rejection by His Father, and a long agonizing death, Jesus endured. He endured and finished the work His Father gave Him to do. He endured perfectly so that we can hold on to hope and not give up in our difficulties. Consider Him and His long-suffering endurance for you, so that you don't grow weary and lose heart.

Let me close this chapter with the Lord's words to Paul in 2 Corinthians 12. It is a perfect reminder to us that we do not wait and suffer alone. We have his all-sufficient grace giving us everything we need.

"My grace is sufficient for you, for my power is made perfect in weakness." 2 Cor. 12:9
Truly, He is all we need. His power shines through our

weakness. His grace and compassion will meet us right where we are in our waiting. Don't grow weary! Run your race with endurance!

GINGER MILLERMON

CHAPTER EIGHT

A Prayerful Heart

"Continue steadfastly in prayer,
being watchful in it with thanksgiving." Col. 4:2

"In my pursuits to be near God, I often forget His desire to be near me.
As much as I long to be in fellowship with Him, He wants it more.
It's His will for me to dwell in His presence and everything He allows me to experience
on this earth—the good and the bad—is to point me to Him."
Katie Orr, "Everyday Faith: Drawing Near to His Presence"

A dear friend called me one evening about some really difficult things going on in her life. It had been a horrible day for her, full of hard decisions and heartache. I listened and told her I was so sorry and gave her a few minutes of advice. After we hung up, my heart heavy for her, I went to the Lord for her family and fell asleep. I woke up early the next morning with her situation on my mind, hoping my words the night before had been helpful to her and not burdensome. But as I began to pray for her again, I was struck with a realization. I hadn't even offered to pray with her over the phone! I had tried to give her godly advice…but I forgot the one thing I could've done that would have been the most helpful and brought the most comfort. My eyes stung with tears of disappointment with myself that I had forgotten to pray *with* my friend, not only *for* her. Why is that not always my first response? We have access directly to the throne of God. We have the attention of the Most High. And we forget! My pastor's wife once said when teaching on prayer,

"Praying with someone is like grabbing their hand and taking them
right to the throne!" Kris Goertzen

It's true, isn't it? We have the profound privilege to go
directly to the throne room of heaven, right to our loving
Father with all the burdens of our hearts, and we forget. We
have the ability to be comforted, to minister, and to serve
others in a way so beyond anything our puny little minds and
efforts could offer, yet often we don't.

This chapter is not meant to heap a load of guilt on you,
revealing the failures of your prayer life. I think if we are
all honest, every last one of us would admit we don't pray
enough...we would probably all concede our prayer life is
pretty anemic. We already know that, don't we? Rather than
a guilt trip, I hope this chapter will be an encouragement and
reminder of the great privilege we have in prayer, and the
great things God does through prayer.

Prayer works. God hears us when we call to Him. I will
never forget the way God heard and answered our cries as
young parents standing over our dying son's bed—when
there was no hope left and nothing else to do but pray. When
trials and circumstances in my life seem hopeless, my mind
often returns to the impossible things God has done in Jarrott's life. It encourages me and reminds me to never give up
and keep on praying!

I grew up hearing the stories of the great missionary, pastor, and orphanage founder, George Müller. I loved to listen
in wonder at the amazing accounts of his complete reliance
on God when circumstances seemed impossible. George
was a man terribly burdened for the orphans starving on the
streets of London, and he opened several orphanages to help
them. It is said his orphanages housed more than 10,000 orphans in his lifetime. And yet he never once asked for money
to feed and clothe the children. He simply took their needs to
his Father. A website dedicated to the life and work of George
Müller, states the following:

"When Müller started the Children's Homes his primary objective was not the welfare of the children. His main concern was that it should be seen that God was providing all the needs as a result of prayer and faith, without anyone being asked or approached." mullers.org

George was convinced that God would have absolutely no problem providing and that he could, indeed, simply take his needs and requests to the throne and God would hear and answer. Yes, he wanted to serve and help the children. But far beyond that, he wanted to serve and help the body of Christ as a whole, showing them God's faithfulness to provide and answer prayer.

On one well-documented morning, George's 300 orphans awoke to no food in the home. They were hungry, ready for breakfast, and there wasn't a scrap of food in the house. Not concerned, George had the children sit and wait at the table, already set with silverware for breakfast. There was no money for food and no one but God knew about their need. Shortly after the children were seated, there was a knock at the door. The baker stood there with baskets of bread and explained that he had woken in the middle of the night with a pressing burden to bake bread for the children. Barely had he left when another knock sounded at the door. The milkman's truck had broken a wheel right outside of the orphanage. He wondered if they could use the milk since he wasn't going to be able to get it delivered. The children had all they needed for breakfast, and of a more eternal impact, they saw first-hand God's miraculous answer to prayer on their behalf.

It is not enough to begin to pray, nor to pray aright; nor is it enough to continue for a time to pray; but we must pray patiently, believing, continue in prayer until we obtain an answer. George Mueller

It fills our hearts with hope for us to hear these accounts of God's faithfulness and answered prayer! It is good to look back in our own lives and remember the ways He has heard and answered our needs.

Right after Joel and I were married, we moved to Colorado where he had an internship with the youth in his home church. After nine months, the internship ended and we moved back to Kansas City so I could finish my Bible College degree. Those were some lean, lean times for us! Joel was working maintenance in a hospital, refereeing basketball games at night, and I was going to school full-time. We were struggling to make ends meet. One day in particular stands out to me all these years later. The bills had piled up and we were very short that month. I was close to reaching full-out panic one afternoon when the mail came. Unexpectedly, there were two checks in the mail. One came from a gentleman in the church where Joel had interned. He explained we were on his heart and he was praying for us and wanted to help us out a little. The other check was from someone Joel had worked for months before as a favor and he didn't even expected payment. Combined, those two checks paid our bills exactly to the dollar. Both checks were mailed at different times, from two people in different parts of the country who had no idea of our need. They didn't need to know...because God knew. I don't remember exactly, but I'm pretty sure I was not in a calm, "bring-it-to-the-Lord-and-lay-it-down" frame of mind. I think I was more in the "panicked-pleas-for-help-and-trying-to-figure-it-out-all-on-my-own" mode. I still do that too often. But God graciously and patiently provides and reminds me of Who He is and what He can do.

I know you have stories of your own answered prayers you can pull from your memory and revisit. I encourage you to do it! Do it often, and do it with others, especially your kids and loved ones observing your life. They need to hear and see the great God of heaven answer prayer. They need you to teach them the importance of taking your needs directly to the Lord, instead of worrying and fretting. And much like the prayers of David, what an encouragement for others to see you hoping and waiting in eager expectation for

Him to answer.

> "O LORD, in the morning you hear my voice;
> in the morning I prepare a sacrifice for you and watch." Ps. 5:3

> "For God alone my soul waits in silence; from him comes my salvation. For God alone,
> O my soul, wait in silence, for my hope is from him. Trust in him at all times,
> O people; pour out your heart before him; God is a refuge for us. Selah." Ps. 62:1,5,8

> "By awesome deeds you answer us with righteousness, O God of our salvation,
> the hope of all the ends of the earth and of the farthest seas;" Ps. 65:5

> "Come and hear, all you who fear God, and I will tell what he has done for my soul.
> I cried to him with my mouth, and high praise was on my tongue. But truly God has
> listened; he has attended to the voice of my prayer." Ps. 66:16, 18-19

Not only are we uplifted by David's prayers, in Scripture there are countless amazing stories we can look to about ordinary people exemplifying hearts of prayer.

Let's start with the story of Hannah in 1 Samuel. Hannah was barren, unable to conceive, and desperately wanted to be a mother. Her husband, Elkanah, loved her dearly, but she longed to hold a child of her own. Being barren in Old Testament times was a sign of disgrace, failure, and embarrassment. Hannah was surely looked upon with disdain or at the very least, pity. To make matters worse, Elkanah had a second wife, Peninnah, who was quite fertile and had plenty of children. Peninnah cruelly gloated over all of her children, and provoked and irritated the childless Hannah.

Year after year, Hannah and her husband went to Shiloh to worship and offer sacrifice to the Lord. Year after year, Hannah begged and pleaded for the Lord to open her empty womb. She continually brought her heartache to God. She believed with all of her heart that God could open her womb and give her children. So she faithfully prayed. In fact, one year at Shiloh, Hannah was especially filled with anguish.

She sobbed in desperation, her lips moving in prayer with no sound. The scene was so dramatic that Eli, the priest, confronted her and accused her of being drunk! Can you imagine? You're coming before the Lord in honesty and agony, pouring out your heart, and you're falsely accused of being a drunk. Poor Hannah! It seemed like she couldn't win! I have been in that desperate place, haven't you? I've been broken on the floor before the Lord, anguish and grief shredding me. Times when the words don't come and all I can do is cry out for help. It is a tremendous blessing to know that during those moments when we are empty and too devastated to pray, the Holy Spirit is praying and interceding for us.

"Likewise the Spirit helps us in our weakness. For we do not know what to pray for as we ought, but the Spirit himself intercedes for us with groanings too deep for words."
Rom. 8:26

What precious hope and comfort that thought should bring to our burdened souls! Our Comforter is praying for us when we have no words of our own.

God heard Hannah's desperate pleas that day. His ears were not deaf to her cries. He had a plan already in motion that she could have never imagined. Once Eli understood her heart and her prayer, he blessed her, and told her to go in peace. Scripture says, when she heard Eli's words of blessing, she went on her way with her face no longer downcast. Her burden had been lifted. Within a short amount of time, Hannah was expecting a baby, many years' worth of prayers finally answered. Her precious son, Samuel, was anointed and appointed by God to be Israel's last judge and a great prophet. Hannah could have had no idea what God was doing. She had no way of knowing if His answer was no, or a delayed yes. But she didn't give up! She persevered in prayer all those years. And the answer to her prayers was beyond her wildest dreams. Hannah is a beautiful role model for us. Don't give up! Persevere in prayer!

And then there's the story of Moses. Maybe the first thing that comes to mind about Moses isn't his prayer life. Probably what comes to mind is his short stint as a baby floating on the Nile bundled in a basket, rescued by Pharaoh's daughter. Or maybe what occurs to you is his leadership of the Israelites during the time of the plagues in Egypt, or his bringing the Ten Commandments down the mountain, or leading over a million people into the desert. He was an amazing man and leader, no doubt. But did you know he was an incredible interceder for the Israelites?

Think about it for a moment. When Moses led all those people from Egypt, they were completely dependent upon God. Moses led them according to God's plans and the people listened to him. Well, actually, they listened for a while… until things got tough. And then they started to whine. Even though God faithfully protected them and provided for them, meeting their every need, and even some of their selfish wants, they still complained. Turn only one page in your Bible in the book of Exodus from the moment they are praising God for His miraculous delivery at the Red Sea, and you will find these ungrateful people complaining! The water at Marah was gross so they complained. God fixed the water and once again provided. Only a few chapters later, the people are again complaining at the lack of water. Instead of asking God, trusting Him to provide like He always had, they griped! The people of Israel whined about the food, complained about Moses' leadership, and rebelled against both Moses and God on multiple occasions. Can you even imagine a million people complaining to *you*? What an awful burden!

And yet Moses' faithful prayers saved Israel on several occasions as he interceded even for the people who were rebelling against him, praying for his enemies. After his own brother led the people in idolatry, Moses pled with God to not destroy the people. Moses interceded for *millions*, and God listened. Doesn't that encourage you to persevere in prayer for that one person on your heart…or perhaps the many people in your life who need Christ? It gives me great hope in prayer! We should never give up taking our requests to Him.

What about when things genuinely seem impossible? When it almost seems like there's no point to prayer...when our hearts think surely this problem is too big for God? It seems like that would be the case in Acts 16 when Paul and Silas are beaten and thrown into prison. They were simply sharing the gospel as God had called them to do, when they encountered a demon possessed slave girl. Paul cast the demon out, and her owners were furious! They had absolutely no regard for this girl's wellbeing; she was only a means to an end for them. Her masters used her to tell people's fortunes and made loads of money off of the poor girl. When Paul freed her from the demon, their source of income shriveled up. In a rage, they incited the crowd against Paul and Silas and had them dragged to the marketplace, stripped and beaten. Soon, they were locked in prison, their feet in stocks. It appeared their preaching career in Philippi was over.

Now at this point, I'm not sure what I would be thinking and feeling. I'm pretty sure I would be extremely discouraged and most likely whiney. Not Paul and Silas! They decided to host a prayer and worship concert. Instead of complaining and wallowing in despair, they lifted their voices to pray and sing hymns. Think of the testimony to the jailer and other prisoners! They saw the peace, strength, and power of Christ flowing from these men. Their prayer and worship time ended in an earthquake, their chains being broken, and a terrified, repentant jailer asking how to be saved. We never know who is watching our response through a trial! I wonder if the story would have ended differently if they had complained in bitterness instead of having an attitude of prayer and peace. Their response challenges me deeply.

I stumbled upon another perfect illustration of a seemingly hopeless scenario in 2 Chronicles. I was reading through the Bible one year when I came upon this story. I

had read through the Bible several times, but I never remembered reading this account before that moment! How does
that happen? I think it's wonderful how God's Word impacts
us differently at different times and seasons of our lives. Now,
this is a story about a man who was not one of the heroes
of the faith or as well known as some in the Old Testament.
He wasn't perfect by any means, but he certainly had a remarkable moment of going immediately to God when circumstances were imploding around him. This is the story of
Jehoshaphat the King of Judah.

Judah was a small country. While Israel boasted ten
tribes, Judah had only two tribes. They were small but they
had a king who longed to serve the Lord. In fact, right before
disaster struck, King Jehoshaphat had gone among the people and appointed Levite priests to administer the law. He
worked tirelessly to turn the nation back to the God of their
fathers and commanded them to fear the Lord and serve
faithfully. That is the setting for 2 Chronicles 20.

The kingdom was peaceful, the king was faithful, and the
priests were warning the people to turn from sin. Sounds ide-
al, doesn't it? Sounds like God should bless the ever-loving
socks off of Jehoshaphat and his people. They were obeying,
doing the right thing! Shouldn't life be smooth and carefree?

2 Chronicles 20 opens with these words: "After this." After what? After appointing priests, after going among the
people to call them back, after telling the people to "Live
wholeheartedly in the fear of the Lord."

"After this the Moabites and Ammonites, and with them some of the Meunites,
came against Jehoshaphat for battle." 2 Chron. 20:1

What? Three different nations were ganging up against
little Judah! In fact, Jehoshaphat's men went on to tell him
exactly where the armies were, and they were descending on
them hard and fast! The nation was faced with disaster and
probably complete annihilation. There was absolutely no way

that Judah could survive against three armies. Jehoshaphat's response is beautiful. Instead of full-blown panic or giving up in defeat, Jehoshaphat did the one thing that could actually make a difference. He prayed.

> "Then Jehoshaphat was afraid and set his face to seek the LORD and proclaimed a fast throughout all Judah. And Judah assembled to seek help from the LORD; from all the cities of Judah they came to seek the LORD." 2 Chron. 20:3-4

I actually prefer the New International Version for verse three. I think it captures the moment.

> "Alarmed, Jehoshaphat resolved to inquire of the Lord..." 2 Chron. 20:3a NIV

I love his initial response! It is an immediate resolve to take his problem to his great problem-solving God. Jehoshaphat knew his nation's only hope of survival would be a miraculous delivery by Jehovah Himself. Realistically, what would it look like in our lives if we were facing a disaster of this magnitude? Phone a friend, email the prayer chain, call your mom, and then blurt out the whole mess on Facebook, Twitter, and Instagram for the entire world? Oh boy...too many times in my life it looks like, "Alarmed, Ginger resolved to inquire of everyone else before the Lord..."

Now hear me: godly friends are good, a mother's advice is priceless, the prayer chain is a wonderful tool, social media...honestly, we could all survive without it...but that's not the point. While those resources are a blessing, they are not THE resource! Our first response should always be to inquire of the One Who loves us and knows us best!

I love Oswald Chambers' thoughts on prayer.

> "We tend to use prayer as a last resort, but God wants it to be our first line of defense. We pray when there's nothing else we can do, but God wants us to pray before we do anything at all. Most of us would prefer, however, to spend our time doing something that will get immediate results. We don't want to wait for God to resolve matters in

His good time because His idea of 'good time' is seldom in sync with ours."
Oswald Chambers

True words, aren't they? God was *not* Jehoshaphat's last resort. In fact, not only did Jehoshaphat go right to the Lord in prayer, he called his people to come together, proclaiming a fast for all the land. And the people came. From every corner of their kingdom, every town in Judah, they flocked to hear what their king would say. Jehoshaphat stood before them, in the courtyard of the temple, and he prayed. He started his beautiful prayer with praise by proclaiming God's power and might. He recounted God's faithfulness through the ages to His people. It was only after he brought worship and thankfulness of God's previous deliverance, that Jehoshaphat brought his very pressing need to the Lord.

What an example for us! How often do we come to God with our need, our list of wants, and our panicked requests for rescue, without ever acknowledging His faithfulness to us thus far? How often do we throw our requests up to Him without a word of praise and thanksgiving?

Jehoshaphat concluded his prayer with these heartfelt, humble words,

"...for we are powerless against this great horde that is coming against us. We do not know what to do but our eyes are on you." 2 Chron. 20:12

Oh, I have lived those words, haven't you? When all seems impossible and I can only cry out, "God, I don't know what to do! But my eyes are on You!"

Jehoshaphat finished his prayer and the whole assembly stood there in stone-cold silence. All the men, with their families, stood waiting. I picture those men of Judah, clutching the hands of their little ones with tears streaming down their faces, begging God in their hearts and minds, to spare their families. They know their wives and children will be slaughtered, or worse, taken and abused by the invading armies.

They have no other hope, no where else to turn, so they wait in silence for God to answer.

And answer He did! Almost immediately, the Spirit of the Lord came over a Levite named Jahaziel and he began to speak God's Words to them!

> "And he said, "Listen, all Judah and inhabitants of Jerusalem and King Jehoshaphat: Thus says the LORD to you, 'Do not be afraid and do not be dismayed at this great horde, for the battle is not yours but God's. You will not need to fight in this battle. Stand firm, hold your position, and see the salvation of the LORD on your behalf, O Judah and Jerusalem.' Do not be afraid and do not be dismayed. Tomorrow go out against them and the LORD will be with you." 2 Chron. 20:15

Don't you wish God would answer all your prayers that quickly? Not only did He tell Jahaziel to tell the people twice "not to fear or be dismayed," He also literally laid out the battle plan of the invading army. God told them not to worry because *He* would be fighting the battle for them. He clearly laid out His plan and assured them of His deliverance.

What great advice for us in the battle! We should not be dismayed or fearful, because the battle is not ours! We don't face our trials alone because we have a God who goes before us. We may not be facing a literal army of soldiers, but we fight daily in a raging war of fear, trials, temptation, sin, and a spiritual enemy who hates us. Remember, we have a roaring lion seeking to devour us! We need to recognize that the battle is not ours to face alone. W need to ask God for His help in our daily struggles.

Jehoshaphat's story doesn't end with God's assurances. It continues with the king taking God at His Word and moving forward in faith. In fact, when most kings would have been sharpening swords and scheming "Plan B" in case God didn't follow through, Jehoshaphat appointed a worship team to sing at the head of the army!

> "...he appointed those who were to sing to the LORD and praise him in holy attire, as

> they went before the army, and say, "Give thanks to the LORD,
> for his steadfast love endures forever." 2 Chron. 20:21

Wow! I have to say, I might have been a little nervous to be on that particular worship team! But what a beautiful story of trust! How often I make "Plan B" for God and try to figure things out on my own. Jehoshaphat simply took God at His Word. The chapter goes on to recount the incredible victory God brought about for His people, completely fighting their battle, and erasing the enemy armies. This incredible, true account has too many intricate details to include in our short pages together. Please take time to read the whole chapter and study all the facets of the way God delivered His people once again. Your heart will be so blessed!

Not only are we encouraged and challenged by these accounts of those who have gone before us, we are also commanded to have a life of prayer. Prayer is an act of obedience. God calls us to pray many times in His Word. Prayer allows us to communicate with God, to worship Him, to confess our sins, and to seek His wisdom and guidance.

> "Rejoice in hope, be patient in tribulation, be constant in prayer." Rom. 12:12

> "Praying at all times in the Spirit, with all prayer and supplication. To that end, keep alert with all perseverance, making supplication for all the saints." Eph. 6:18

> "Continue steadfastly in prayer, being watchful in it with thanksgiving." Col. 4:2

> "Pray without ceasing, give thanks in all circumstances;
> for this is the will of God in Christ Jesus for you." 1 Thess. 5:17-18

> "First of all, then, I urge that supplications, prayers, intercessions,
> and thanksgivings be made for all people." 1 Tim. 2:1

Those verses only scratch the surface of what God says about prayer. We are commanded to pray. Pray for repentance for our own wicked hearts, pray for God to help us love Him more, pray for each other, pray for the lost, pray in our trials, and pray in every circumstance. Simply pray always. The God Who sent His beloved Son as a sacrifice to rescue our condemned souls from hell, longs for us to come to Him in prayer and fellowship. Prayer is an unmerited privilege. He truly cares about every single need that weighs on our hearts. There is nothing more important in our day than planned, quiet time talking to our Savior. He hears, He listens, and He answers. Spend time with Him today. He longs for you to come.

Jesus: Our Perfect Prayer Warrior & Intercessor

When the cross was looming only hours before Jesus, knowing the agony of His upcoming crucifixion, the terrible separation from His Father that He would endure, Jesus was praying for us. (John 17:20-25) Moments before walking into the Garden of Gethsemane where He would be arrested and taken to die, Jesus was looking to heaven and thinking of us. That blows my mind!

Jesus had a very active prayer life. Maybe we think because He was God in the flesh that He didn't need to pray. But Jesus truly took upon Himself our fragile humanity. He depended on His Father every day, exactly as we do. He felt hunger, grief, temptation, trials, loneliness, anger, and every emotion and experience we feel, yet without sinning. He faced it all, which is why He is the perfect High Priest for us. He understands our weakness, frailty, trials, and temptations. He went to His Father for strength every day. Jesus spent time separating Himself from people—and even from His disciples—to find quiet places to pray. Quiet places to talk with His Father. He prayed not only to communicate with His Father but also to be an example for us.

"And after he had dismissed the crowds, he went up on the mountain by himself to pray. When evening came he was there alone." Matt. 14:23

"But he would withdraw to desolate places and pray." Luke 5:16

"In these days he went out to the mountain to pray,
and all night he continued in prayer to God." Luke 6:12

"And rising very early in the morning, while it was still dark,
he departed and went out to a desolate place, and there he prayed." Mark 1:35

If the sinless, holy Son of God found it important to pray, how much more should we? We, who are fallible, imperfect, weak human beings, need desperately to have time alone with our Father! Jesus perfectly shows us the importance and necessity of prayer.

Not only is He our example in prayer, He is our mighty prayer Warrior, our Great High Priest, our tireless Intercessor for us to the Father. In Old Testament times, the high priest would enter the Most Holy Place to make intercession and sacrifice for the people's sins. But even that high priest could only enter that sacred place once a year. A curtain separated the Holy Place and the Most Holy Place. When Jesus went to the cross as our final and ultimate sacrifice, that curtain tore in two and we are no longer separated from coming directly to our Father. Jesus entered that inner sanctuary on our behalf and He has become our High Priest forever. He is always in God's presence and continually interceding for us.

"...he is able to save to the uttermost those who draw near to God through him,
since he always lives to make intercession for them." Heb. 7:25

Remember, as in Job's story, Satan goes before God and accuses His children. Satan's very name means "accuser." But those accusations hold no merit in heaven because Jesus paid it ALL at Calvary! Our sins are covered and His righteousness is imputed, or ascribed, to us. We have become the righ-

teousness of God because Christ took our unrighteousness
from us and gave us His perfect holiness. (2 Cor. 5:21) Not
only do we have His imputed righteousness, but when Satan
accuses before the throne, Jesus is right there every second
making intercession and praying for us!

The Apostle Paul says it perfectly:

"Who is to condemn? Christ Jesus is the one who died—more than that, who was
raised—who is at the right hand of God, who indeed is interceding for us." Rom. 8:34

Who, indeed, can condemn? No one! Because there is
no condemnation for the ones who are in Christ. (Rom. 8:1)
Those are some of the most beautiful words in Scripture to
me. Because the veil has been torn, and our High Priest has
gone before us, we can confidently and boldly approach the
throne of grace. We don't need any other mediator, priest, or
intercessor. Jesus took care of all of that. We can come freely
to our Father and receive His grace and comfort.

"Let us then with confidence draw near to the throne of grace,
that we may receive mercy and find grace to help in time of need." Heb. 4:16

What an undeserved, amazing privilege we have in
prayer. Don't neglect it. Come freely and come often! You
will certainly receive grace to help in your darkest times of
need.

"When a Christian is weak, and can hardly pray for himself,
Jesus Christ is praying for him..." Thomas Watson

CHAPTER NINE

A Servant's Heart

"This is how one should regard us, as servants of Christ and stewards of the mysteries of God. Moreover, it is required of stewards that they be found faithful." 1 Cor. 4:1-2

"God puts you in hard moments when you cry out for his comfort so that your heart becomes tender to those near you who need the same comfort." Paul Tripp

As we endure trials, we have a unique and privileged opportunity to grow in our compassion and sensitivity toward the needs of others, and to be more useful servants for the Kingdom of God. Think about it for a minute: if you have never been through a trial, never known grief and suffering, never felt the confusion and pain of plans and lives gone awry, how will you ever relate and sympathize with those who are suffering? Hard times in our lives give us a season of time to cultivate sensitivity in our hearts and teach us to serve others better.

Some people are natural-born servers, overflowing with mercy and compassion for others. They have the ability to quickly see a need and know exactly what to do to meet that need, and they delight to do it. Serving is not a burden to them. The rest of us have to learn by experience and let the Lord soften and refocus our self-centered hearts.

My parents are both compassionate, natural servers. It is amazing to watch them each in action. My mom's efforts have focused mainly on her family, and I have been blessed to be on the receiving end of her kindness and thoughtfulness for years. Many, many times we have come home from a long weekend of ministry or an extended tour, and we walk through the door to find the house cleaned, laundry done, and something delectable in the crockpot. During these ongoing months of my illness, she has been a constant source of help and encouragement to our family. She sees what needs to be done, whatever would be the most helpful, and does it, simply to be a blessing. That's my mom's servant heart. She doesn't need attention or praise, doesn't need others to notice and shower her with accolades, in fact she prefers that they don't say anything. She simply loves to serve.

My dad is blessed with the same gift of serving but is wired a little differently. He truly doesn't know a stranger and is constantly helping people. It doesn't matter if it's someone he met the moment before or even someone he has only heard about, if there's a need, he will try to meet it.

One occasion stands out to me from several winters ago. I was having a coffee date with my dad at a favorite local spot on a bitterly cold day. We were visiting over steaming mugs of coffee, looking out the picture window, and watching people. A man in the parking lot caught my eye as we were talking. He was moving with an uneven gate, and seemed to be in a hurry. He started waving his arms frantically, and I realized he was trying to flag down the local transit bus and let them know he was coming. Unfortunately, he didn't make it in time, and the bus flew by without slowing. The man's shoulders slumped and he haltingly kept walking, trying to cross the busy street. My dad's back was to the man and he missed the whole thing, but he noticed the dismayed look on my face. I sadly explained that the disabled man had missed his bus. I hadn't even finished the story when my dad leaped up, threw a dollar down for his coffee, and called over his shoulder,

"Don't worry! I got it! I'll take him where he needs to go!"

And out the door he sailed.

I sat back in amusement, cradling my hot coffee, and watched the show begin. As the man hobbled across the busy intersection, dodging traffic, my stout little dad ran across the parking lot, calling for him. I don't know if the man was partially deaf too, but he never heard my dad. Next thing I know, my dad is dodging traffic and chasing him down. I see my dad smile and gesture and point the man back to the coffee shop. They carefully made their way back across the street (I was still thoroughly entertained at this point) and got into my dad's car and drove away. He called me later to tell me all about his new friend.

As I sat in that cozy coffeehouse, the thought occurred to me that I was so blessed to share that moment with my dad. So blessed, to see once again, his servant's heart in action. My response was feeling bad for the man, a feeling of mercy and empathy. My dad's response was pure compassion resulting in a beautiful moment of sacrificial servanthood. Mercy and empathy are wonderful qualities, but they are a little different than compassion. Mercy feels something, sympathizes even, but doesn't necessarily take action. Compassion sees a need, suffers with the other person, and seeks to do something about the need. It is an action. A heart of compassion for someone is more than a feeling—it requires a response.

What does it look like practically to learn to have a servant's heart? Like I said, for some it doesn't come naturally. It may not be our spiritual gift. But that doesn't excuse us from stepping outside of what comes naturally and comfortably for us and being obedient to God's Word. There are many aspects of living the worthy life we have been called to live that don't come easily. Among many other commands, we are instructed to forgive, love, be patient, kind…and serve. I don't think *any* of these come naturally. We are selfish beings by nature, aren't we? A prayer of our hearts should always be that God would open our eyes to see the needs around us! We must pray that He would help us to daily deny ourselves in order to seek the good of others first.

It's a difficult thing to wrap our minds around, serving others when we are in the thick of battle ourselves. When our own situation is overwhelming, usually the last thing on our mind is serving someone, or meeting someone else's needs. Yet that is often exactly what would help us the most. It is so easy to get discouraged and depressed when we are wrapped up in and focused on our own issues. When we can't see through the fog of our unpleasant or perhaps tragic circumstances, we lose perspective. I'm not saying there's isn't a time to step away and heal, or take a break from certain responsibilities as we deal with hard things in our lives. I have been there. I have had seasons of needing to get my spiritual life in order and taking time to heal from heartbreaking trials. But even in those most desperate of times, we can still serve, even if it's a little less hands-on or from a distance. We can still pray from a sickbed, send a note or text of encouragement, or pick up the phone and make a call. We can and should make an intentional effort to see beyond our own little world and cultivate a heart for others. Our command to serve one another doesn't come with an exception clause.

"Therefore encourage one another and build one another up…" 1 Thess. 5:11

"Bear one another's burdens, and so fulfill the law of Christ." Gal. 6:2

"…through love serve one another. For the whole law is fulfilled in one word: "You shall love your neighbor as yourself." Gal. 5:13b-14

What does building each other up and bearing each other's burdens look like in our daily life? It means suffering with someone, and sharing in their grief and sorrow. Bearing someone's burden means we aren't afraid to jump into his or her mess and get our hands dirty. It's not easy or pleasant sometimes to be with someone who may not share our joy for life at the moment, but that's when they need love and

encouragement the most!
Remember,

> "...encourage the fainthearted, help the weak, be patient with them all."
> 1 Thess. 5:14

We can tend to get impatient with people who are struggling. Especially if we have never walked in their shoes and experienced their circumstances. There is certainly a time to gently and lovingly share hard truths or carefully reprove someone who can't seem to see beyond today or get out of the pit of despair. But I think the key here is the "gently, lovingly, and carefully" part of sharing our thoughts. Some of us, who see things very black and white and didn't get overloaded with the gift of mercy, need to take a lesson on gentleness and compassion. We are clearly told to patiently encourage, uplift, and bear the burdens of the weak and fainthearted.

Remember Job's friends? They were horrible at this! They sat for a little bit with him at first, and then when they opened their mouths, most of what came out was merciless, harsh judgment. They would have been much better off to sit in silence. It would have been an encouragement for Job to simply have his friends there, grieving with him. Sometimes that is the most comforting thing we can do for someone. There are times when a long hug, a willingness to sit in silence, and simply being present can be far more helpful than words. We usually can't "fix" someone's circumstances, but we *can* lead them to the hope of Scripture, give them godly advice, and encourage them. We can bear them up and fulfill Christ's command to love each other.

I was talking to my father-in-law recently about this quality of being a faithful servant. He and my mother-in-law both epitomize this characteristic, having served tirelessly in the same small church in Colorado for forty-five years. That's a long time to love on the same people and community! They have been a tremendous role model and example of life in ministry to our family. As we were visiting, my father-in-law reminded me of the story of two elderly sisters who attended his church for many years. The sisters had been born during the Great Depression and had several siblings. Their father, looking for work, had left their home in North Dakota and traveled to Oklahoma to work in the oil fields. As soon as possible, their mother and all the kids traveled south to join him. Tragically, they hadn't been in Oklahoma long when their father was killed in the fields. The family found themselves fatherless and destitute. Not knowing what else to do, their mother packed up the large family and started the long journey back North. The girl's uncle lived in North Dakota and when he heard about their dire situation, he made a life altering, unbelievably sacrificial decision. He was engaged to be married and had recently finished building a home for his soon-to-be-bride. Instead of marrying the love of his life and starting a family of his own, he broke off his engagement and took in his sister and all of her children. He raised those kids as his own and provided for them until they graduated from high school and got jobs of their own. He never married. That, my friends, is an unprecedented act of sacrificial servanthood.

The biblical story of Ruth has a similar tone of selfless sacrifice and love. Ruth was a Moabitess who married into a Jewish family from Judah. She was accepted and loved by her in-laws, Elimelech and Naomi, even though historically there was enmity between Judah and Moab. As the story unfolds at the beginning of the book of Ruth, Elimelech and both his sons all tragically die. Naomi, Ruth, and another daughter-in-law, Orpah, were left as destitute widows. It was a horrible thing to be a widow in the ancient world. Often these women were forgotten or ignored, relying on family to care for them. Since the elderly Naomi was from Judah and had no family in Moab, she decided to move back home perhaps to see if any of her relatives were still alive. She selflessly encouraged her two daughters-in-law to stay in Moab where there would be a good possibility they could find new husbands to care for them. There would be little hope of a husband for them in Judah. Orpah agreed to stay in Moab with her people, but Ruth would not leave Naomi. There was nothing Naomi could say or do to convince Ruth to stay. Ruth absolutely could not imagine neglecting her beloved mother-in-law. Listen to Ruth's determined, passionate words to Naomi:

"But Ruth said, "Do not urge me to leave you or to return from following you. For where you go I will go, and where you lodge I will lodge, Your people shall be my people, and your God my God. Where you die I will die, and there will I be buried. May the LORD do so to me and more also if anything but death parts me from you.""
Ruth 1:16-17

Ruth refused to desert Naomi. She insisted that she would leave her people, her gods, her family, and friends, and everything she knew to keep caring for Naomi. She understood if she went with Naomi, that she would probably never remarry, would likely be shunned by the people of Judah, and would remain childless and destitute. It didn't matter to Ruth. She was committed to faithfully serving Naomi at great personal loss and difficulty. What a beautiful picture of sacrificial love! If you've read the book of Ruth, you know how her seemingly hopeless situation dramatically turns into a tender love story. A story of provision and redemption only a loving God could orchestrate. And that destitute Moabitess woman ends up in the direct lineage of the Messiah! Wow! Aside from the lesson of being a faithful servant, Ruth's story is one of such redemption and hope. You never know what amazing plans God has up His sleeve! Nothing —and no one—is beyond His redeeming love!

I'm most impacted by Ruth's story knowing that she was a grieving widow. She had lost her husband. And yet she still had eyes to see someone else's needs. She was willing to look beyond her own devastating circumstances and serve Naomi. She could have curled up into a little ball in despair or run home to her parents. Instead, she fully embraced the most difficult choice, the least comfortable and secure plan. She willingly gave up her hope of a future to ensure that Naomi would have provision. Having a servant's heart is not easy. Being a servant and loving others sacrificially is especially trying when you're dealing with your own hardships. I came across a quote that reminds me there is no "perfect" time or place to serve.

"He who does not serve God where he is would not serve God anywhere else."
Charles Spurgeon

When I consider someone who was always willing to serve both God and his fellow man, I think of the apostle Paul. That man never quit serving other people, championing the cause of Christ, and tirelessly spreading the gospel! In fact, he referred to himself as a servant of Christ (Phil. 1:1; Rom. 1:1; Titus 1:1). "Servant" (the Greek word doulos) literally means slave, a person who is owned by an individual. Paul was honored to wear this title (Gal. 1:10; Titus 1:1). It is the Old Testament picture of a slave who, out of deep love, commits himself to his master for the rest of his life (Ex. 21:2–6). Paul felt privileged to be a servant of Christ. I think he looked at serving his Master as the greatest privilege in life. He was joyful in serving Christ and ministering to unbelievers even when it meant suffering severe persecution. In the book of Philippians, written from a Roman prison and often called the book of joy, Paul is grateful that his trials had served to further the gospel. Everyone knew he was in chains for Christ, and he was thrilled that his chains were prompting his fellow believers to speak more boldly (Phil. 1:12-14). Because Paul viewed himself as a servant of Christ, he considered everything he endured to be for the purpose of bringing glory to God and advancing the good news to the lost. Paul's whole identity was in being a slave of Christ. What an amazing servant of God! Oh, that I would for even

one day consider myself only a slave of Christ! Instead of remembering I am a servant of Christ, too often I find myself
in slavery to my possessions, my "me time," my emotions, my
busyness, and my sin. Everything else in life can get in the
way and we forget that when we are children of God, we are
servants of Christ. Like Paul, it is our identity, our privilege,
and our responsibility.

"This is how one should regard us, as servants of Christ and stewards of the mysteries
of God. Moreover, it is required of stewards that they be found faithful." 1 Cor. 4:1-2

We are servants and it is required that we be found faithful. Faithful to serve and love others, faithful to use what God
has invested in us. He has entrusted us with the mysteries of
God! I am reminded of the parable of the talents in Matthew
25:14-26. The master in this parable was going on a long
journey, and he called three of his trusted servants in for a
meeting before he left. He gave them each a sum of money to use and invest while he was gone. He expected them
to use it wisely until he returned. When the master at last
came home from his journey, he called his servants together
to hear a report of how they had used his resources while
he was gone. The first two servants were excited to report
that they had doubled the money their master had left them!
They had been faithful to invest and work hard while the
master was gone. The master was thrilled with their report.
He commended them and put them in charge of far more of
his resources. He even invited them to share in his joy and
happiness. Then the third servant came to the master. I imagine this servant must have been cowering in fear and shame,
sweating bullets at what he had to report. Unlike the first two
servants, he had *not* been a faithful steward. He had no heart
for his master's kingdom, instead his focus was on serving
himself. He made the lame excuse to his master that he was
afraid to invest what had been left to him. He had instead
buried the money in a field, keeping it safe until the master

returned. He handed that one small sum of money back to his master. He had done nothing...no investment, no work, no effort for the kingdom.

Understandably, the master was furious! He recognized the false excuse and called his servant what he was...wicked and lazy. He took the money and gave it to the others who had invested wisely and threw that unwise servant out of his kingdom. This parable, and a similar one in Luke 19, describes the two attitudes we can have as we await Christ's return. We can be faithful to use what He has invested in us, sharing the gospel, serving others, working for the kingdom. Or we can be exactly like that wicked, unfaithful servant... unwilling to work, self-centered, and lazy.

Much has been invested in us! Christ died to redeem us! God has given us everything we need for this life and its trials, for godliness, and holiness (2 Pet. 1:3). We have all that we need to serve Him faithfully. We have no excuse. Our time, our resources, our talents, our money are not ours. We are stewards of what God has given us. So what are we doing with His investment? God has given us each a testimony, a story of His salvation and faithfulness. Are we sharing it? He has given us each spiritual gifts and talents. Are we using them for His glory and the building up of His church, or for our own boasting and glory?

He has given us each twenty-four hours in every day. Where do we invest our time? Is it in others or only for our own self-interests, self-promotion, and entertainment? Maybe it is time for us to take a long examination of our priorities and hearts to determine if we are being faithful servants. Serving is not an option, it is a command and a requirement when Jesus is our Master. Our efforts should advance *His* kingdom, not our own glory and good. Jesus is coming back! No one knows the time or date, but He will come (Mark 13:32). This life is a mist. We will soon vanish, and our time here will be over (Jas. 4:14). What have you done with your short visit here? Will you be found faithful?

As faithful stewards, we must serve diligently and compassionately, giving our very best in whatever He has called us to do. Many of us have jobs to make a living and provide for our families. It's part of life, right? Then you serve God faithfully in the workplace, looking for every opportunity to show love, mercy, and compassion to the lost. You look for every window to share the gospel. You seek to be the best employee your boss has ever hired...not to bring glory to yourself but to magnify the name of Christ. If you're a stay-at-home momma, you serve your husband and children in love and dedication as if you are serving Christ Himself. You bear your family up and are long-suffering and kind. If you're a student, be the best student you can possibly be, and serve God faithfully in school. You let God's glory and goodness shine through you so that everyone knows you are His! Whatever walk of life or season you are in, simply serve. "Give of your best to the Master," the old hymn writer so eloquently said.

I have heard so many people say they aren't qualified to serve. They say they need to grow in their walk before they serve or that God would never want to use them because of their scarred past. Those are nothing but lame excuses. God will use every single one of us who are seeking Him and are willing to be used...from the youngest child to those in their sunset years.

"Whatever you do, work heartily, as for the Lord and not for men, knowing that from the Lord you will receive the inheritance as your reward. You are serving the Lord Christ." Col. 3:23-24

We have the opportunity to serve and worship Christ Himself with every deed, every kind word, and every act of compassion. And it is amazing how the seemingly smallest outreach of kindness is an incredible blessing to someone who is hurting.

I am reminded of a sweet moment with our daughter

McKenzie that I was privileged to observe when she was about twelve years old. Our family was doing ministry at Word of Life Inn in Schroon Lake, NY for the summer, and new guests would come weekly for us to serve. Every week I would give a concert for the guests. One week I noticed an older gentleman with his leg in a full cast, confined to a wheelchair.

I had barely finished my concert and sat down when McKenzie leaned over and whispered to me, "Mom! There's an old guy in the back in a wheelchair. I know exactly how that feels. I have to go talk to him after the service!"

And as soon as the last "amen" was said, off she went. You see, McKenzie had been born with extra bones in both her feet. She lived in extreme pain, until we finally discovered the problem when she was in middle school. At the beginning of her sixth-grade year, she had double foot surgery and was confined to a wheelchair or crutches for many long months and continued to live in pain. She understood the frustration and misery.

All through that week, when other kids were racing around, playing games, McKenzie could be found sitting and chatting with that man. They laughed as they shared tricks to scratching an itch under a cast, and she gave him all the advice she could. I don't think any of us understood the impact her simple kindness made until the end of the week. The man's wife came to me in tears and shared that they had been coming to the camp for many, many years. Her husband had an accident right before their trip and was so discouraged and depressed, he almost hadn't come. She told me that McKenzie's sensitivity and kindness had made it one of the best weeks at the conference center the man had ever experienced.

One of the important things about suffering is that it gives us the ability to understand others' suffering. How can we understand if we have never suffered? And if we never suffer and have affliction in our lives, how will we know the comfort and grace that our Father will lavish on us in our deepest need?

"Blessed be the God and Father of our Lord Jesus Christ, the Father of mercies and the God of all comfort, who comforts us in all our affliction, so that we may be able to comfort those who are in any affliction, with the comfort with which we ourselves are comforted by God." 2 Cor. 1:3-4

We are comforted by God in our affliction and can in turn comfort others with the comfort we have received from Him. Those hard moments in life can be used to cultivate compassion in our hearts and use what we have learned to comfort the hurting people around us.

"Everything I endure is designed to prepare me for serving others more effectively. Everything." Chuck Swindoll

It doesn't take much to serve someone, does it? A bright smile, a look of understanding, a long hug, a meal, a bag of groceries, a card, or simply a commitment to pray. Every one of us has everything we need to serve each other out of a deep love for our Master. We are called to serve the poor, the orphan, the widow, the helpless, and our neighbor. And every time we serve another, we are directly serving Him. Are you being faithful to serve?

"And whoever gives one of these little ones even a cup of cold water because he is a disciple, truly, I say to you, he will by no means lose his reward." Matt.10:42

Jesus: the Perfect Servant's Heart

"For even the Son of Man came not to be served but to serve, and to give his life as a ransom for many." Mark 10:45

It doesn't take more than a few minutes of reading through the Gospels to see Jesus' servant's heart of compassion. He was constantly moved with compassion while gazing out over the masses that followed Him. Whether the people were lepers, hungry, demon possessed, diseased, crippled, blind, or burdened by great sin, Jesus loved and healed with tremendous mercy.

"When he saw the crowds, he had compassion for them, because they were harassed and helpless, like sheep without a shepherd." Matt. 9:36

"When he went ashore he saw a great crowd, and he had compassion on them and healed their sick." Matt. 14:14

Clear back in Isaiah it was prophesied that He would lovingly serve and protect as a shepherd loves His flock.

"He will tend his flock like a shepherd; he will gather the lambs in his arms; he will carry them in his bosom, and gently lead those that are without young." Is. 40:11

He is, after all, the Good Shepherd (Heb. 13:20; 1 Pet. 5:4; Jn. 10:11). And a good shepherd loves and tends to his sheep, protecting, feeding, and providing for their every need. Every day of His ministry here on earth, Jesus served. The King of Kings did not come to be served, even though He deserved to be exalted and worshipped. He came to serve and to give His life as a ransom for all (Mark 10:45).

One of the most beautiful displays of Jesus' humble servanthood came only hours before His crucifixion. Satan had already entered Judas' heart, and Jesus knew He was about to be betrayed and given over to be killed. As He and His disciples sat at the Last Supper, Jesus suddenly arose, wrapped a towel around His waist like a slave, and began to lovingly wash His disciples' feet. This act of lowly servanthood completely shocked His disciples! In fact, Peter pulled away in horror at the thought of His Master washing his filthy dirt-streaked feet. Jesus was giving them a picture of true humility that they would take with them for the rest of their lives.

He was showing them the importance of serving one another, modeling the attitude of having no hesitation to do the lowliest of jobs. And they would need this example, as they would move fully into a life of service after Jesus' death and resurrection. Jesus commissioned His disciples to go out and serve with humble abandon, and He expects no less from us. And how could we do any less when we consider all He has done for us?

"Do nothing from selfish ambition or conceit, but in humility count others more significant than yourselves. Let each of you look not only to his own interests, but also to the interests of others. Have this mind among yourselves, which is yours in Christ Jesus, who, though he was in the form of God, did not count equality with God a thing to be grasped, but emptied himself, by taking the form of a servant, being found in human form, he humbled himself by becoming obedient to the point of death, even death on a cross." Phil. 2:3-8

Our Jesus, the suffering Servant, in great humility, emptied Himself and gave His all for us. In an attitude of gratefulness and obedience, our own hearts should be stripped of pride and self, and instead be filled with humility, putting others' needs and interests ahead of our own. Please pray with me that He would open our eyes to see the needs of those who cross our paths and that He would give us hearts to serve. Oh, that we would love others in His strength and with the depth of His tireless compassion!

Give of Your Best to the Master
By Howard B. Grose
Public Domain

Give of your best to the Master;
Give of the strength of your youth.
Throw your soul's fresh, glowing ardor
Into the battle for truth.
Jesus has set the example,
Dauntless was He, young and brave.
Give Him your loyal devotion;
Give Him the best that you have.

Give of your best to the Master;
Give of the strength of your youth.
Clad in salvation's full armor,
Join in the battle for truth.

Give of your best to the Master;
Give Him first place in your heart.
Give Him first place in your service;
Consecrate every part.
Give, and to you will be given;
God His beloved Son gave.
Gratefully seeking to serve Him,
Give Him the best that you have.

Give of your best to the Master;
Naught else is worthy His love.
He gave Himself for your ransom,
Gave up His glory above.
Laid down His life without murmur,
You from sin's ruin to save.
Give Him your heart's adoration;
Give Him the best that you have.

CHAPTER TEN

A Heavenly-Minded Heart

"For our light and momentary troubles are achieving for us an eternal glory that far outweighs them all. So we fix our eyes not on what is seen but on what is unseen, since what is seen is temporary, but what is unseen is eternal." 2 Cor. 4:17-18

"If you read history you will find that the Christians who did most for the present world were just those who thought most of the next." C.S. Lewis

During the darkest seasons of my life, I have found great comfort in knowing this world is not all there is for me. It is a temporary home that will fade like the sun breaking through the fog, and I am only here for a brief moment in comparison to eternity. Life is so hard. If I didn't know that there was a purpose for my life and that this short stint on earth would end with the promise of eternity with Jesus, I think I would have given up a long time ago! Think about it. What would be the point of collecting stuff, accumulating things, working hard, suffering hardship, and then after a life quickly gone by...it ends in death and into the dirt we go. But praise God this isn't all there is! This is only a brief work trip until we get to the joy of our real home in heaven.

We have probably all had those times when we were far from everything familiar, longing for the comfort and security of home. I know I certainly have! At four years old, Jarrott was an inpatient at Kennedy Krieger Institute in Baltimore, connected with Johns Hopkins University, and he and I were stuck there for two torturous months, 1,276 miles from home. He had recently had his tracheotomy removed, still took all of his calories via gastrointestinal tube, and needed to learn to eat by mouth. The program at Kennedy Krieger was eight weeks, and Jarrott and I braced ourselves for long days full of therapy. I slept curled up in a pullout chair in Jarrott's hospital room next to his bed. On the other side of a thin curtain, we shared the room with a little boy who screamed much of time, and his parents fought nearly every minute they were together. Need I say more? It was not a fun time.

But by far, the worst part for me was being disconnected from my family by the distance. This was all before affordable cell phones, Facebook, or Skype. I only had a few phone cards people had given us as gifts, and I carefully rationed the minutes on my calls home to Joel and the kids. While I was caring for Jarrott's needs in Baltimore, Joel and our other precious kids were twenty hours away at home. McKenzie and Brennan were six and four years old and I would be almost physically sick with longing for them and Joel. About three weeks in, I had a complete meltdown and almost checked Jarrott out of the program and headed home. Joel talked me down from that figurative ledge, and I knew I had to do what was best for Jarrott long-term. Nearly ten long, grueling weeks finally passed before we were released from the hospital. Other than my week-three meltdown, I had more or less held myself together, tried to make the best of it, and counted the days until we could go home. The Lord was very near and faithful, and His Word gave me the strength I needed. I resolved to keep telling myself it was temporary. Temporary circumstances, temporary housing, temporary separation.

Joel came to pick us up and we made the long drive home. I will never forget the warm spring evening when we at last pulled up to our house. I nearly jumped out of the car before it stopped. All I could think about was holding my kids. I ran up our sidewalk, the kids ran toward me, and I was overcome. I dropped to my knees, scooped them up, and began to sob. I'm talking about the turn-your-face-inside-out, ugly cry. The dam broke and all of the longing, all of the sorrow, the separation, and heartache flooded out of me, and sweet relief and joy took its place. It was over. Home at last!

I look back on that overwhelming sense of relief of coming home, and I eagerly anticipate and wonder what it will feel like to finally be…*HOME*. To be swept into heaven's gates and Jesus' arms and to know that the suffering, the separation, the longing for *Him* is over. To know I am done with the sin and cares and tears of this world. I don't long for Home enough. I get so caught up in the trappings and dramas of this short life and I forget this isn't it. This is only temp housing, and there is so much more to come!

"We look not to the things that are seen but to the things that are unseen. For the things that are seen are transient, but the things that are unseen are eternal."
2 Cor. 4:18

It's not an easy task to fix our eyes on the things to come instead of what's directly in front of us. Our "light and momentary troubles" as Paul calls them in 2 Corinthians 4, don't feel light and momentary in the least! They seem heavy and endless. This life and its burdens, heartaches, and trials can seem like the end game. But it's all in our perspective, isn't it? When Joel was a youth pastor, he used to use an illustration with our teens giving a visual picture of eternity.

He would hold his fingers in the air about an inch apart. "This," he would say, "is your life right now. That's it…this tiny little inch represents your whole life from beginning to end." He would let that sink in for a second and then point his other arm straight out in the opposite direction. "Eternity is forever that way. Forever. Your life here on earth is this tiny speck in comparison to all of eternity. What are you going to do with the little bit of time that you have here? How you live your life matters for eternity."

We forget, don't we? This little inch of time we have on

earth is nothing compared to the glories that await us at our final destination. We are simply travelers here, passing through on our way to a home far superior.

It always challenges me to read the great faith chapter, Hebrews 11, and remember all of the Old Testament men and women who recognized that they were only sojourners on this earth. They lived completely by faith, without the comfort and aid of the Scripture that we are privileged to have today, and they kept their eyes fixed on their eternal home. After commending such men as Abel, Noah, Enoch, Abraham and more, the writer of Hebrews speaks of their heavenly focus.

> "These all died in faith, not having received the things promised, but having seen them and greeted them from afar, and having acknowledged that they were strangers and exiles on the earth. For people who speak thus make it clear that they are seeking a homeland. If they had been thinking of that land from which they had gone out, they would have had opportunity to return. But as it is, they desire a better country, that is, a heavenly one. Therefore God is not ashamed to be called their God, for he has prepared for them a city." Heb. 11:13-16

This world is not our home. There is a better country waiting for us. We have a place prepared for us where there will be no more sorrow, no death, no sickness, and no sin (Rev. 21:4). Like the great men and women in Hebrews 11, we strive to live by faith, not by what we presently see, knowing our true hope is laid up for us in heaven (Col. 1:5).

Truly, we are strangers and aliens here, longing for our homeland, but we often live as if this is our permanent home. We put our efforts, our focus, and our resources solely toward making this life comfortable and perfect. It's like staying a week in a hotel room in a foreign country and using all of our own efforts and resources to repaint, hang pictures, lay down new carpet, and make it comfy and beautiful, only to leave it all a few days later! It makes no sense, does it? Yet, that's how we live when we forget our citizenship, when we become earthly-minded instead of heavenly-minded. We have to stop trying so hard to fit in here, because this isn't where we belong!

I recall being in India for our adoption and feeling completely out of place. Everything was foreign to me. I wasn't comfortable, and with the danger surrounding us, I really wanted to simply blend in! The problem was...there was no blending in for this pale, blonde American! I stood out like a sore thumb. I was a traveler, a pilgrim, quickly passing through and longing for my homeland. I was there for a purpose, and my focus and desire was on completing my job and returning home. And believe me, when my feet hit American soil in Chicago, there was sweet joy and relief!

We long to fit in here, to be like everyone else, accumulating stuff and social status that doesn't matter in the end. Remember, we are not earth dwellers! Instead, we fix our eyes on Jesus and what He has in store for us when this short life is over. We don't work to blend in here, we work to make a difference for the Kingdom. We use our time, our resources, and our talents for things that matter for eternity.

That's exactly what Paul was speaking of when he told the Colossians to

"Set your minds on things that are above, not on things that are on earth." Col. 3:2

Paul was reminding the Colossians that they had been raised up with Christ, their old selves had died, and they should seek heavenly things instead of earthly things (Col. 3:1-3). How do we set our minds on what's above? We habitually set our minds, our affections, our resources, and our efforts on heavenly things. We discipline our minds, by the power of the Holy Spirit working in us, to dwell not on what is seen and temporary, but on what is unseen and eternal. Setting our minds on earthly desires is so easy! In fact, it takes no effort at all. It is our natural habit, and it is where our unfettered carnal minds will always go. We have to make an intentional and concerted effort to look to the eternal.

This is especially important when the circumstances and trials of this life overwhelm us. When all we can see are the valleys behind us and the mountains in front of us and the future looks bleak. If life were perfect here, we wouldn't long for home, would we? And so we look beyond our present circumstances and we focus on the hope and glory that awaits us.

One of the most moving events in our ministry happened several years ago at Angola Prison in Louisiana. I had been asked to do a concert for the men, and I have to tell you, I was a nervous wreck! Angola is notoriously one of the worst prisons in the country and houses some of the most dangerous criminals. We really had no idea what to expect. In fact, we told the prison chaplain "no" to his request more than once before Joel and I both became convicted to simply trust the Lord and go. So we went; in fact we spent the night inside the prison grounds as the warden's guests. Some of the inmates even cooked an amazing meal and homemade chocolate chip cookies for us.

The concert that evening ended up being one of the best experiences of our ministry. The men were incredibly respectful and completely focused on worship that night, their hands raised, tears streaming down many of their faces. An amazing time of prayer followed the concert as men streamed forward to accept Christ or request someone to pray with them for their needs. There was genuine peace and joy in that room. It was astounding!

Joel had the opportunity to visit with one of the prisoners who was serving a life sentence for murder. He was only nineteen years old when he killed a man in a drunken bar fight that he didn't even remember. He had probably been in prison for over half of his life, and he would never leave. He had no chance of parole. At some point during his time in Angola, he had heard the gospel and received Christ as his Lord and Savior. His life had dramatically changed! He was a photographer working for the prison's magazine, and spoke with great delight about all that God had done in his life. His words and perspective have had a lasting impact on our lives.

"You know what?" he said to Joel. "When I first came here, I just kept my eyes on those front gates. I was always thinking of life beyond those gates. But since I came to know Christ, I keep my eyes on the pearly gates! I am so thankful that God put me here. I know if I had stayed on the outside, I would be dead by now and in hell."

Wow! What a beautiful, eternal perspective! It took our breath away! How could he be content, happy, and joyful in prison for life? How could he not long for the outside world? He was so grateful that Jesus had saved his soul and that he would spend eternity with Him. His goal in life shifted from getting out to having a ministry and impact right there in prison, reaching souls for Christ while incarcerated. It was his mission field. His is the most poignant testimony I have ever personally heard of "blooming where you're planted" and being used by God wherever you land. He had learned to be content where God had him. Much like the story of Joseph being faithful to be used in prison when Potiphar's wife wrongfully accused him, this prisoner determined to serve God in every circumstance. Most of us will never be in prison or have to face that particular trial. But we create prisons of our own making, don't we? Prisons of sin, unrealistic expectations, and ungratefulness.

Joel and I were struck with the complete contentment of so many of the men we met at Angola. Most were in prison for life. Never would they have the freedom of the outside world, and yet they overflowed with joy and peace. It was incredible! Many men had graduated from seminary while in prison. They were pastors, ministering and sharing the good news to their fellow inmates. Some were even hoping to be missionaries, requesting to be sent to other prisons so they could spread the gospel there.

It puts me to shame! I have every resource, every freedom and convenience, and so often my gaze is on all the trappings of this earth. I find myself discontent with my stuff, and I forget that I am a pilgrim. The decisions that I make, the way I view my trials, and how I use my resources should be different knowing my citizenship is in heaven.

"But our citizenship is in heaven, and from it we await a Savior, the Lord Jesus Christ."
Phil. 3:20

As the apostle Paul wrote those words in Philippians 3, he sat in prison, likely shackled to an imperial guard. His eyes and heart were fixed on the eternal home that awaited him and not on his temporal circumstances. Earlier in this passage, he spent a moment giving his impressive earthly credentials only to follow up with these verses:

"But whatever gain I had, I counted as loss for the sake of Christ. Indeed, I count everything as loss because of the surpassing worth of knowing Christ Jesus my Lord. For his sake I have suffered the loss of all things and count them as rubbish, in order that I may gain Christ and be found in him…" Phil. 3:7-9a

Paul had achieved much in this world. He was a powerful Pharisee, a Roman citizen, and a rising star among the religious leaders before he met Jesus. All of those accolades meant no more than trash to him once he came to Christ. Nothing else mattered to Paul. His eyes were fixed on the prize, and he was running the race with one goal in mind. Focused, determined, and holding fast to the truth he had attained through the gospel. Before his transformation on the Damascus road, Paul's achievements had been all about himself and his own self-righteousness. After his salvation, he realized all of those previous efforts and accomplishments were futile. He needed only Christ's perfect righteousness imputed to him, put on his account. So with the past behind him, and Christ before him, Paul pressed on for the finish line. It is with this thought of straining toward the goal, that Paul reminds us that our citizenship is not on this earth. Instead, it is in heaven, where we will be with our precious Savior, Jesus. And so we fix our eyes on Him. We focus our eyes and our hearts daily on Him, in every circumstance.

Do you remember the story of Peter walking on the water in Matthew 14? Jesus had been on the mountain praying, and the disciples headed out across the sea in their boat. A huge storm had blown up in the night, and the waves were beating against the boat. In the middle of the night, out of nowhere, here comes Jesus, strolling peacefully along the top of the water! Freaked those disciples out! Jesus calmly called out to them, telling them not to fear.

Impetuous Peter, probably speaking before thinking, hollers back that if it's really Jesus, why doesn't He have Peter come on out and walk on the water too? I love Jesus' simple answer to Peter.

"Come."

So Peter hops out of the boat in a raging storm and begins to walk to Jesus, right on top of the waves. How amazing that must have felt for Peter...looking at Jesus across the water, walking to Him, the wind and rain pelting his face. It was going so well at first. And then, Peter started to notice again the wild storm, the violent sea, and the winds whipping around him. He began to look about and felt panic and fear overcome him. And his feet began to sink into the waters!

"Lord, save me!" Peter cried out. Jesus simply reached out his hand and rescued him out of the angry waves and calmed the storm.

Peter lost his focus. He forgot to fix his eyes. When his gaze and trust were on Jesus, he was surviving the raging sea, walking right through the fury of the storm. He was obviously walking in Jesus' miraculous strength and not his own. And then he forgot.

That's us, isn't it? We simply forget. Life is hard. But Jesus is everything. He is enough. He is all. In trials, in despair, in prison, in the valley, on the mountaintop... He is all we need. Don't lose your focus. Don't give up. Don't lose heart.

We have His strength for our journey. We have everything we need.

"So we do not lose heart. Though our outer self is wasting away, our inner self is being renewed day by day. For this light momentary affliction is preparing for us and eternal weight of glory beyond all comparison." 2 Cor. 4:16-17

"His divine power has given us everything we need for a godly life through our knowledge of him who called us by his own glory and goodness." 2 Pet. 1:3 (NIV)

Jesus: the Perfect Heavenly-Minded Heart

Everything about Jesus' earthly life pointed toward heaven. From His teaching in the Sermon on the Mount, to some of His last words on the cross to the thief dying next to Him, Jesus spoke of heaven. He instructed His disciples and all who would listen, that they should store up treasures in heaven, not on earth. He promised that He was going to prepare a place in His Father's house and would come back for His own.

Jesus knew His time here on this earth was short. Surely that fact must have been at the back of His mind at all times. He never got caught up in the trappings of His culture, the material possessions He could have accumulated. He was here for only one purpose. He was here to die to rescue and redeem us from the slavery of our sins. But until that time was fulfilled, until God's preordained moment that Christ would suffer on the cross, He lived sinlessly to be our example in every way. He walked here perfectly so that His perfect righteousness could be imputed to us. He was reviled, rejected, and misunderstood even by His closest friends. He had nothing of His own, not even a place to lay His head. His focus was always and only to please His Father and to fulfill God's will. His goal was to make disciples who would spread the gospel to all the nations of the world after His death and resurrection.

Jesus is our perfect example of a heart and mind focused on what truly matters for eternity. He has walked before us through trials, pain, loss, and excruciating hardship and death. He endured beautifully and perfectly in our place.

As we close our time together, dear friend, remember who you are. If Jesus is your Lord and Savior, you are His precious, beloved, adopted child, and you do not walk this journey of life alone. If you aren't absolutely certain of your relationship with God, please go back to Chapter Two—the very end of the chapter—and read again about Jesus' surrendered heart for us, and how you can know Him as your Savior. There is absolutely nothing more important in this life. Make sure of your salvation!

When you are His, the Holy Spirit, the Comforter, resides inside of you, your faithful High Priest intercedes for you, and your heavenly Father bends His ear toward you. The darkest night, deepest crevice, strongest storm, or farthest reaches of the earth cannot hide you from His loving grace and care. You are His and He is with you always. You are never alone. You have everything you need.

"May our Lord Jesus Christ himself and God our Father, who loved us and by his grace gave us eternal encouragement and good hope, encourage your hearts and strengthen you in every good deed and word." 2 Thess. 2:16-17 (NIV)

Saved by Grace
By Fanny Crosby
Public Domain

Some day the silver cord will break,
And I no more as now shall sing;
But oh, the joy when I shall wake
Within the palace of the King!

And I shall see Him face to face,
And tell the story—Saved by grace;
And I shall see Him face to face,
And tell the story—Saved by grace.

Some day my earthly house will fall,
I cannot tell how soon 'twill be;
But this I know—my All in All
Has now a place in heav'n for me.

Some day, when fades the golden sun
Beneath the rosy-tinted west,
My blessed Lord will say, "Well done!"
And I shall enter into rest.

Some day: till then I'll watch and wait,
My lamp all trimmed and burning bright,
That when my Savior opes the gate,
My soul to Him may take its flight.

DISCUSSION QUESTIONS

Chapter 1:

1. What trials do you find yourself facing as you begin reading this book?

2. What is the most difficult trial you've ever endured?

3. How have you seen God work in your life through suffering?

4. Is there a time in your life or the life of a loved one when God has used trials to bring you closer to Him? Spend time in prayer today laying your trials and burdens at the foot of the cross.

Chapter 2:

1. In studying the account of Cain and Abel, what "little" sins or temptations in your life come to mind that have the potential to grow out of control? (For example, Cain's bad attitude and jealousy evolving into murder.)

2. Have you ever felt alone or abandoned, as Joseph must have felt? Were there people in your life who came alongside you to help? What are some Scripture verses or passages that were especially comforting to you?

3. What is that one thing or circumstance in your life that you need to surrender? Are you willing to have a "How can I serve you here, God?" attitude, even in the hardest moments?

4. Has there been a time in your life when you called on the name of the Lord to be saved and surrendered your life to Him? Describe that time and how it has changed your life. Take time today to thank Him for His saving grace!

Chapter 3:

1. Tell about a time when you struggled to forgive. Are you still wrestling with that situation?

2. After studying Joseph's story, are you challenged to make the conscious and deliberate choice to forgive?

3. As you've grown in your walk with Christ, have you learned to "cover offenses" as Prov. 17:9 says? Do you see the importance, especially in marriage and in close relationships, to stop bringing up old offenses and to truly forgive from the heart? What does that look like for you?

4. Take a moment to pray through the situations in your life that you are reluctant to let go of and forgive. Ask God for His help to release anger, bitterness, and unforgiveness. Pray specifically for the person who has hurt, betrayed, or offended you.

Chapter 4:

1. What trial or situation is happening right now in your life that is making it hard to give thanks?

2. The story of the ten Lepers is personally very moving and convicting to me. How often I have forgotten to thank God for answered prayer! Are there times that come to mind when you have neglected to give thanks for His provision and care?

3. Do you struggle to find joy in your life? Are you always complaining, never content? How do you think this affects your testimony to others? Do the people in your life see the joy of the Lord in you? Evaluate what you are relying upon to bring you joy.

4. Take extra time today to dwell on the gospel and the beautiful reality that when you receive Christ, you are rescued from death and adopted into His kingdom. Make the decision to incorporate thanksgiving into your daily prayer life. Start today!

Chapter 5:

1. Tell about a time when you had to use self-control and take your thoughts captive, choosing to dwell on the commands of Phil. 4:8. (Thinking on things that are true, honorable, just, pure, lovely, commendable, excellent, and praiseworthy.)

2. Do you struggle regularly with fear, worry, and anxiousness? If so, how do you deal with your fears?

3. Do you consider worrying to be sin? As "deep-seated distrust of the Father" as Charles Trumbull says? Are you letting your circumstances and emotions control you instead of Who God is? Confess your lack of trust and ask God to help you.

4. Our hearts are prone to wander and forget the goodness and provision of the Lord—that "spiritual amnesia" we all wrestle to overcome. Take time today to declare and remember specific provision and care that God has provided to you. Thank Him for His faithfulness.

Chapter 6:

1. Tell about a time when something seemed completely hopeless in your life.

2. What do you tend to place your hope in the most? (For example, finances, relationships, job, etc.)

3. What are some of your favorite promises from Scripture that bring you comfort and hope in times of distress? What biblical stories encourage you personally to hang on to hope?

4. Spend time in prayer bringing your seemingly hopeless situation to your Heavenly Daddy today. Remember, He will turn His ear to your cry and hear your every need. His arms are open wide!

Chapter 7:

1. Share a circumstance that required a difficult season of waiting. How did you handle it?

2. Do you struggle to "be patient with everyone" as we are commanded in 1 Thess. 5:14? Who do you tend to be impatient with in your life? Do you need to meditate through Proverbs to see God's specific words about impatience and anger? Would your family call you a patient and kind person? Are you a blessing to your family, or are you tearing down your home with impatience?

3. How can you have peace in the waiting? First of all, I challenge you to do some self-examination. Are you spending quality time in God's Word, memorizing and reviewing the truths of His assured faithfulness to you? Are you revisiting the biblical stories and accounts of those who have gone before you who experienced God's faithfulness and

deliverance? What are some Scriptures or thoughts in this chapter that have encouraged and challenged you to run with endurance and wait patiently on the Lord?

4. Take time to pray for His help in building patience in your life—both with people and circumstances. Ask the Holy Spirit to both convict your heart and give you grace to patiently wait on God's timing in your life.

Chapter 8:

1. Discuss a time when God very specifically and clearly answered your prayers. It's so important to revisit those answered prayers and remember God's faithfulness!

2. What biblical account encourages you to persist in prayer? Do you sometimes feel like Hannah, pleading with the Lord for years to have your need answered?

3. What keeps you from prayer? What distractions consume you that keep you from finding time to pray? What practical steps do you need to take to eliminate those distractions?

4. The account of Jehoshaphat greatly encourages me to take every need directly to the throne, before taking it to everyone else. What need in your life do you perhaps need to talk about less to others and more to the Lord? How can you make this a pattern in your life?

5. Friend, don't use prayer as your last resort...make it your first response in time of need. Today, spend time in prayer... about prayer. Ask for God's help to strengthen your prayer life, so you can be "constant in prayer." (Rom. 12:12) Remember, as you pray, Jesus your great High Priest is praying and interceding for you!

GINGER MILLERMON

Chapter 9:

1. Have you been through a change or situation in your life that suddenly gave you compassion for others in a new or dramatic way? (For example, cancer or illness, loss of a job, death of a loved one, a prodigal child.)

2. Do you have the gift of serving? Does serving come naturally for you or is it quite an effort to see others' needs and respond? If it doesn't come naturally, after reading this chapter, do you see the importance of letting the Lord soften your heart and open your eyes to the needs around you?

3. Is there someone in your life that is an example to you of a servant's heart, like my parents are to me? What have you learned from them and how can you implement that practice? Give some practical ways that you can serve others in your life.

4. We are servants, and it is required that we be found faithful. Jesus is our ultimate example of servanthood, and He has given us everything we need to live godly lives and be faithful servants. Are you using what He has invested in you? Pray for wisdom, strength, and a desire to serve others well.

Chapter 10:

1. Has there been a time when you have been far from home for an extended period of time and longed for your family and home? Describe the feeling of homesickness you felt. Have you ever longed for your heavenly Home?

2. It's so easy to set our minds on everything we see before us...all of the earthly enticements. How can you set your mind on things above?

– 170 –

3. There will always be times in our lives when our priorities need to shift and change. Times when we forget this world is not all there is for us... Remember, it's temp housing! How are you doing with remembering this world is temporary and your permanent home is still to come? Are there some priorities that need to change in your life?

4. Spend some time in prayer thanking the Lord that this world is not all there is for us. There will be an end to our sorrow, tears, and tribulations. Ask Him to help you focus your heart and mind on things above and not on the fleeting attractions of this world. Be encouraged! Take heart! This life is but a mist, and soon we will rejoice and worship in our real Home!Notes:

NOTES

Chapter Two: A Surrendered Heart

[1] Wiersbe, W. W. (1993). *Wiersbe's Expository Outlines on the Old Testament* (Ge 4:1–5). Wheaton, IL: Victor Books.

[2] Edersheim, A. (1997). *Bible History: Old Testament* (Ge 37–39). Oak Harbor: Logos Bible Software.

[3] Edersheim, A. (1997). *Bible History: Old Testament* (Ge 37–39). Oak Harbor: Logos Bible Software.

Chapter Nine: A Servant's Heart

Witmer, J. A. (1985). Romans. In J. F. Walvoord & R. B. Zuck (Eds.), *The Bible Knowledge Commentary: An Exposition of the Scriptures* (J. F. Walvoord & R. B. Zuck, Ed.) (Ro 1:1–7). Wheaton, IL: Victor Books.

Chapter Ten: A Heavenly-Minded Heart

Wiersbe, W. W. (1996). *The Bible exposition commentary* (Col 3:4b). Wheaton, IL: Victor Books.

GINGER MILLERMON is a nationally recognized songwriter, recording artist, gifted communicator, and speaker for concerts, women's conferences, and special events. She has garnered multiple "Top 10" inspirational singles and is in demand as a concert vocalist, speaker, and worship leader. She has an incredible testimony of God's faithfulness to her family that is chronicled in her book *Grace Thus Far*. Ginger's music and testimony have been featured internationally on many television and radio programs including Focus on the Family, the 700 Club, and 100 Huntley Street.

A graduate of Calvary University with a degree in Biblical Studies, Ginger and her husband, Joel, have been in ministry together for over twenty years. They reside in the sandhills of Kansas with their four children.

To order Ginger's CDs or books, for more information on her music and speaking ministry, or to book Ginger for your event, please visit www.gingermillermon.com

GINGER MILLERMON

Made in the USA
San Bernardino, CA
16 April 2018